IN THE FOOTSTEPS OF
ALEXANDER

IN THE FOOTSTEPS OF
ALEXANDER

THE KING WHO CONQUERED
THE ANCIENT WORLD

MILES DOLEAC

METRO BOOKS
New York

METRO BOOKS
New York

An Imprint of Sterling Publishing
387 Park Avenue South
New York, NY 10016

Editorial and design by
Amber Books Ltd
74–77 White Lion Street
London N1 9PF
www.amberbooks.co.uk

Project Editor: Michael Spilling
Designer: Jeremy Williams
Picture Research: Terry Forshaw

ISBN: 978-1-4351-5375-2

For information about custom editions, special sales, and premium and corporate purchases,
please contact Sterling Special Sales at 800-805-5489 or specialsales@sterlingpublishing.com.

Manufactured in China

2 4 6 8 10 9 7 5 3 1

www.sterlingpublishing.com

CONTENTS

INTRODUCTION   6

ALEXANDER'S RISE TO POWER   16

KING ALEXANDER III: THE JOURNEY BEGINS   36

WAR WITH PERSIA   54

FROM ISSUS TO GAUGAMELA   84

THE REWARDS AND COSTS OF CONQUEST   112

TO INDIA, BABYLON AND BEYOND   140

ALEXANDER'S CITIES   178

THE KING IS DEAD. LONG LIVE THE KING(S)   212

MAP: THE EMPIRE OF ALEXANDER THE GREAT, 334–324 BCE   218

HOW DO WE RETELL ALEXANDER'S STORY? THE SOURCES   220

SELECT BIBLIOGRAPHY   221

INDEX   222

PICTURE CREDITS   224

Introduction

In 336 BCE, Philip II of Macedon, the man Greek historian Diodorus Siculus called 'the greatest of the kings in Europe', was assassinated, ostensibly by internal enemies, having united the ever-belligerent Greek city-states (with the exception of Sparta) under his leadership. He was preparing to undertake a bold war on Achaemenid Persia, to avenge at long last the sacrilege that Xerxes (r. 486–465 BCE) had wrought upon the Greeks and their temples a century and a half earlier (Diodorus XVI.95.1). The League of Corinth, the coalition of allied Greek powers, had conferred upon Philip the title of *strategos* ('supreme commander') and given him unlimited power to lead an invasion of Asia and Persia's mighty empire. But, when Philip fell under the blade of Pausanias, a member of his own royal bodyguard, in the autumn of 336, leadership of the impending Persian campaign passed to his 20-year-old son, Alexander, and the course of Western history was likely changed significantly as a result.

The young Alexander was no novice on the battlefield. He had commanded Philip's left flank at the Battle of Chaeronea in 338 BCE at which the Macedonians (and their Thessalian allies) defeated an alliance of Greek city-states led by Athens and Thebes to become the effective masters of Greece.

Alexander was said to have broken the lines of the Theban 'Sacred Band'. Numbering around 300, the Sacred Band was made up of pairs of male lovers, bound together by personal affection, loyalty to one another and the honour of their city-state. They had defeated the mighty Spartans decisively at Leuctra in 371, but they were no match for the then 18-year-old Alexander, who seemed to possess an uncanny, natural gift for finding the precise moment and place to launch a decisive assault against the enemy. Even at this early stage in his career, he led his troops personally; he took exactly the same risks that he asked of them.

A Wealthy Kingdom

But the story of Alexander begins before Chaeronea. It begins in and with Macedon, the fertile, timber-rich region north of Thessaly (and the Greek city-states), into which flows the Haliacmon and Axios rivers. The political

Right: Bust of Philip II, King of Macedon (r. 359–336 BCE), father of Alexander.

Facing page: 'Xerxes at the Hellespont' by Jean Adrien Guignet. Xerxes set out in 480 BCE with a fleet and army which Herodotus estimated was roughly one million strong.

boundaries of the 'kingdom of Macedon' – that is the Macedonian 'state' that, ruled by Philip's Argead Dynasty, came to dominate first the Balkans and, thereafter, the Greek city-states to the south – shifted throughout antiquity, but, topographically, the area under control of the Macedonians was a roughly uniform circuit of mountainous highlands that enclosed river basins and fertile plains. By the standards of central and southern Greece, Macedon was a land replete with natural resources. Generous rainfall coupled with flowing rivers, abundant timber forests and significant reserves of precious metals helped not only to make Macedon independent and self-sustaining, but made the Macedonian kings desirable, even necessary, trading partners for the Greek city-states. The Athenians, in particular, needed Macedonian timber to construct the triremes

Right: Gold larnax or small coffin designed to hold human remains (either cremated or bent into position). This elaborately-ornamented larnax was unearthed at Vergina (in ancient Macedon) and may have contained the remains of Philip II himself. It bears a decorative sun, possibly a symbol of Philip's Argead Dynasty or a nod to Zeus-Helios, master of Olympus and god of the firmament.

that would become so critical to the Greek defence against Persia in the early fifth century BCE and to the rise of Athens' naval-based empire in the latter. The wily Perdiccas II (r. 448–413 BCE), king of Macedon during much of the Peloponnesian War, had managed, by alternating alliances with Athens and Sparta, to guarantee Athenian dependence on Macedonian timber along with a nearly unending influx of Athenian silver in exchange for it. Philip II's expansion of Macedon's political boundaries in 356 BCE brought the rich veins of silver and

gold from the mines of Mt. Pangaeum into the Macedonian orbit, providing yet another boost to the kingdom's already robust royal economy. The ornately-adorned Macedonian royal tombs unearthed at Vergina (ancient Aegae, Macedon's first royal capital) provide indisputable evidence that the kings of Macedon had become very rich indeed in the course of the fifth and fourth centuries BCE. At the height of his powers, in the greater Mediterranean world, Philip's wealth would have been matched only by that of the Great King of Persia. It was the Macedonian royal house's significant wealth and resources that allowed the kings to engage in a delicately non-committal, diplomatic dance with Greece's main warring powers – Athens, Sparta and Thebes – for nearly a century and a half as they weakened one another to Macedon's ultimate benefit.

Greeks or Non-Greeks?

Scholars have long sought in vain to answer definitively the question of whether or not the Macedonians can properly be characterized as 'Greek'. Were they a tribal people akin to the Dorians who migrated into and settled on the Greek mainland in perhaps the twelfth century BCE, the future Macedonians choosing instead

to remain in the highland regions of the extreme north? Were they an indigenous Balkan people more closely related to the neighbouring Illyrians and Thracians? Could their ancestors have been wandering Mycenaeans, Homeric Agamemnons displaced by the Dorians and settling, bent but not broken, in the timber-laden north in the hopes of regaining their footing there? The history of early Macedon is shadowy indeed. All of the above remain mere hypotheses, intelligent guesses, but guesses nonetheless. There is such scant evidence of the Macedonians' original language that it is, in fact, impossible to say with any certainty what Macedonian ethnicity was. Furthermore, early Macedon's archaeological record (c. 1200–650 BCE) is so spotty that definitive evidence of even permanent settlement has not yet been found and precious early tomb finds are devoid of inscriptions that could reveal whether the Macedonians were using a language separate from Greek.

It is at least possible that, when the Macedonians proper do emerge into the light of history around the middle of the seventh century BCE, they could claim some relationship, if not direct descent, from Greeks of the northwestern mainland. The house of Philip II traced its roots to Argos (hence, 'Argead') and to the greatest of the Greeks' heroes, Heracles, although there is no firm linguistic or archaeological evidence to support Herodotus' report that the first Argead king, Perdiccas I, had migrated north to

Left: The ruins of ancient Aegae (modern Vergina), Macedon's first royal capital.

Macedon from Argos near the turn of the eighth century BCE (*Histories* 8.137–139). The archaic poet Hesiod claimed that Zeus had a son named Makednon (whose name means 'tall') who 'rejoicing in horses' dwelt around Pieria and Mount Olympus (*Catalogue of Women*, frag. 3), from whom the Macedonians possibly took their name, although some scholars have argued that a *Makedones* (a 'Macedonian') could simply refer to a 'highlander' and not, specifically, a 'son of Makednon'. Indeed, Mount Olympus, the mythic abode of the Greeks' highest gods (and Greece's highest peak) towered above the plain of Macedon in the Pierian range that divided Macedon from Thessaly to the south. The first Argead capital, Aegae, practically lay at the foot of it.

But despite these and other fleeting connections, real or invented, to Greek culture and lore, we cannot definitively label the Macedonians as 'Greeks'. The southern Greeks certainly did not view them in that regard. The Greeks were exclusivist by nature, as was their preferred system of government, the *polis* ('city-state'). Indeed, inhabitants of the Greek city-states saw the Macedonians as uncouth, backwater *barbaroi* ('barbarians'), foreigners, as distinctively 'other' and lesser than themselves.

ARCHELAVS REX.

Apud Fuluium Ursinum in numismate argenteo.

The attempts of Macedonian kings like Alexander I (r. c. 498–454 BCE), who took the nickname 'the Philhellene' ('fond of the Greek'), to ingratiate himself with the Greeks of the south demonstrate a clear distinction between the two peoples. Further, there is evidence that there did exist a unique Macedonian language, or at least dialect, as ancient sources employ a Greek verb, *Makedonisti*, which means something along the lines of 'to speak in the Macedonian manner'. One way or another, the 'highlanders' from north of Greece did not

sound quite like their southern neighbours. There is, however, no doubt that, by the end of the fifth century BCE, standard Attic Greek, even if tinged with a Macedonian brogue, had become the language of the Macedonian court, whether for personal or official correspondence.

But language may have been one of few commonalities that a Macedonian aristocrat shared with, say, an Athenian citizen in the fifth and fourth centuries BCE. Macedonian barons were hard-drinking horse lords often more interested in hunting and fighting than philosophy or theatre, although, as the Macedonians became increasingly enmeshed in Greek politics and trade, they could not resist immersing themselves, to one degree or another, in Greek culture. This was especially true of Perdiccas II's son, Archelaus (r. 413–399 BCE), whose court hosted two of Athens' finest tragic poets, Agathon and Euripides. A little of Macedon's highland culture (and, perhaps, savagery) rubbed off on the latter, for it was at the Macedonian capital, Pella, that Euripides wrote his dark masterpiece, *The Bacchae*, likely inspired by the highlanders' uniquely visceral brand of Dionysiac worship, which, famously, was said to include the handling of live serpents. But despite his affection for Greek (or 'Hellenistic') culture, the manner of Archelaus' death – drunk and run through, whether intentionally or not, by the spear of one of his royal pages, during a hunt – shows him to have possessed purely Macedonian preoccupations, at least in most respects. In general, Macedonians hunted on horseback and used spears and swords

Left: Fourth-century CE Roman mosaic from Halicarnassus (Asia Minor), depicting Dionysus dancing nude with grape-vine crown and leopard. Long before the Romans, the Greeks and Macedonians had associated the god with leopards, which, along with goats and serpents, were Dionysus' principal animal attendants.

to fell their prey. Lions and boars served as the primary, but not the only, targets for Macedonian elites, who frowned upon the use of nets or traps because these devices diminished the difficulty and, by extension, the heroism of the kill. The horse, whose speed and agility were critical to the hunter's success, was a fixture on Macedonian coinage and in the life of every good Macedonian aristocrat. The Macedonians, like their mythic progenitor, Makednon, 'rejoiced' in horses indeed. The value of a good horse and good horsemanship, whether for recreation or war, was ingrained in Macedonian boys from an early age. It was a lesson our Alexander would heed closely.

Alexander's Parents

In July 356 BCE, a 20-year-old Epirote princess, Olympias, having wed Philip II, king of Macedon, less than a year earlier, gave birth to Alexander III, eventually, 'the Great'. Olympias was the daughter of Neoptolemus I, king of the Molossians, a tribe in Epirus, whose dynasty traced its descent to another Neoptolemus, son of the mighty Achilles. Epirus lay between the Pindus Mountains and the Ionian Sea in the northwestern reaches of the Greek peninsula. Philip's marriage to Olympias served to solidify a political alliance between his and Neoptolemus' kingdoms. The battle-hardened Philip was also an astute politician and diplomat, a fact that is sometimes lost amidst his many military innovations and accomplishments. He understood that power could be attained and wielded bloodless and off the battlefield as well as on it. It was for this reason – along with his healthy libido – that Olympias was Philip's fourth, and not his last, wife. So, Alexander was said to be descended on his mother's side from Achilles and, on his father's, from Heracles.

They were not only the two greatest heroes of Greek legend. They were sons of Zeus himself, *hemitheoi* (half-gods), born of the King of Olympus' unquenchable lust for mortal women. When considering Alexander's possible later claims to divinity, it is important to remember that he would have been taught from early on that the blood of the gods flowed through his veins. If we are to believe Plutarch's report, Olympias may even have shared with her son a story that, the night before her wedding to Philip, she was visited by Zeus himself in the form of a thunderbolt (*Life of Alexander* 1.2), the Olympian's preferred method of insemination. As such, the young Alexander may have thought himself closer to Achilles and Heracles than mere distant ancestry. Whatever the case, a deep-seated belief in his divine or semi-divine heritage no doubt accounted, to one degree or another, for the adult Alexander's storied bravado and fearlessness in the face of danger.

Both Alexander's parents bore imposing personalities. Olympias was an initiate, and perhaps a priestess, of the ancient, orgiastic rites of Dionysus, with their ecstatic dances and snake-handling. Plutarch reports that Olympias even tamed and slept with serpentine companions, a fact that finally repelled even the almost preternaturally lustful Philip from her bed. We are told that Olympias pursued the rites of Dionysus more zealously than any woman in the region and, when possessed by the god, her trance-like Dionysiac frenzy was wilder and more terrifying than that of other women, especially to men. Additionally, her savage, if self-protecting, behaviour in the wake of Philip's assassination, murdering her rival, Cleopatra (Philip's last wife), along with the young queen's infant daughter, shows Olympias to have been a woman of indomitable disposition.

For his part, Philip II had come to power in 359 BCE, perhaps after having been first appointed regent to his brother Perdiccas III's son and legitimate heir, the five-year-old Amyntas IV. Whether it was the tenuous situation with the neighbouring Illyrians, who had killed Perdiccas on the battlefield and were threatening Macedon's borders, or the simple matter that Philip had no wish to govern in anyone's name but his own, Alexander's father soon cast aside any appearance of the regency and declared himself the rightful king of Macedon. Rival claimants to the throne rose up to take advantage of an Argead royal house in seeming disarray, one Pausanias, supported by Thrace, and another, Argaeus, by the always-meddling Athenians. Philip quickly dispatched both, buying Thracian loyalty away from Pausanias and falling

Above: Olympias (c. 376–316 BCE), fourth wife of Philip II of Macedon and mother of Alexander. The Macedonian queen is pictured on a Roman gold medallion (third century CE), issued by the emperor Caracalla (r. 211–217), as part of a propaganda campaign wherein the emperor attempted to promote his descent from Alexander.

Right: Fourteenth-century Greek illuminated manuscript, depicting the court of Philip II of Macedon (seated). The young Alexander is depicted (crowned, centre) in both the upper and lower tableaux. In the lower tableaux, Olympias, the Queen, is shown on right, with her attendants.

upon Argaeus in a cunning hit-and-run operation outside of Aegae. History records nothing more of either rival. The Illyrian king, Bardylis, would have appeared a more formidable opponent, but, by 358 BCE, Philip was bold enough to refuse the Illyrian monarch's offer of peace based on the *status quo*. Instead, Philip employed, to devastating effect, a coordinated combination of cavalry and infantry to crush his Illyrian opponents, making himself the chief political power in the region.

In his youth, Philip had been a guest (i.e. 'hostage') in the house of the celebrated Theban general, Epaminondas (c. 418–362 BCE), whose lethal cavalry wedge formation had contributed in no small part to Thebes' rise to prominence and, briefly, dominance among the Greek city-states. Epaminondas was said to have been immediately impressed with Philip and even to have tutored him in military and diplomatic matters. The Theban general was unwittingly sowing the seeds of his city-state's own destruction. Philip was a quick study. In less than two years' time, through skilled diplomacy and military acumen, he had turned dangerous and troubling circumstances – a Macedonian king felled in battle, aggressive enemies menacing on all sides – into a resounding claim of Macedonian dominance throughout the Balkans. The south and Greece was soon to follow. It was with Philip II's Macedon in the ascendancy that Alexander was born.

Facing page: Theban general, Epaminondas, leads his army at the Battle of Leuctra (371 BCE), wherein the Boeotian League (led by Thebes) defeated Sparta and her allies.

Alexander's Rise to Power

'Corresponding to brutishness it might be most appropriate to suggest superhuman virtue: virtue on a heroic or godlike scale; as Homer makes Priam say of Hector that he was exceedingly brave, nor did he seem to be Son of a mortal sire, but of a god. So if, as they say, mortals become gods through heroic excellence (*arete*), the state most opposed to brutishness would clearly be of this kind.' (Aristotle, *Nicomachean Ethics* 7.19-26)

Aristotle, like most Greeks, accepted a basic division between gods and men, but this was not some impassable chasm. The chasm could in fact be bridged by superhuman virtue, by the displaying of what the Greeks called *arete*. Alexander's own heroic ancestors, Heracles and Achilles, had done just this, as had Dionysus, the god to whom Alexander would devote considerable attention later in life. They,

however, had one advantage that Alexander did not enjoy; or at least he did not realize it initially. In all three cases, one parent was an immortal. But this fact was not essential to a mortal man's apotheosis in the fourth century BCE. As early as 477 BCE, the poet Simonides eulogized the Greek hoplites who fell at Plataea as eponymous heroes. Herodotus and Thucydides likewise bear witness that Plataea's honoured dead were granted divine rites and even accorded an annual festival.

City founders commonly received divine honours also. Both the Athenian general Hagnon and the Spartan Brasidas, heroes of the Peloponnesian War, were deified after their deaths and, more notably, the Spartan navarch Lysander was honoured by the Samians during his lifetime,

Facing page: The young Alexander is washed in a basin by a nymph. Late Roman mosaic, depicting the life of Alexander, fourth century CE, Baalbek Odeon (National Museum of Beirut).

Right: Gilded bronze statue of the youthful Heracles, with club and lion-skin pelt, Roman, second century CE.

having his statue placed among those of the gods at Delphi. Lysander, writes Plutarch, was the 'first Greek to whom cities erected altars and offered sacrifices as to a god' while he was still alive (Plutarch, *Lysander* 18.5).

He would not be the last. The difference, perhaps, for Alexander was that, while Hagnon, Brasidas and Lysander were certainly paid divine honours, they did not become fully divine like his own heroic ancestors. They were more like Aristotle's 'gods among men' – greater than the mortals in their immediate vicinity, but hardly worthy to wield the club of Heracles (*Politics* 3.8). Alexander wished to press matters a step further.

A Precocious Prince

In the summer of 356 BCE, the Macedonian prince was born into a world that would allow him to do just that. According to legend, the great Temple of Artemis at Ephesus burned down the night of Alexander's birth, an incident that local Persian priests (*magi*) interpreted as an omen of calamities that would soon befall the mighty Achaemenid Empire. We are not certain that Alexander was the eldest of Philip's sons, but we can say that his only other attested son, Philip Arrhidaeus, was mentally handicapped and considered unfit to rule, at least in comparison to Alexander. As

such, Alexander appears to have been marked out for the succession early on. He was a precocious, intellectually-inquisitive child and a born leader; Plutarch characterizes him as an 'impetuous' and even 'violent' youth. We are told that, at the age of seven, with his father away on campaign, Alexander entertained Persian envoys visiting the Macedonian court and proceeded to interrogate

Above: Alexander's great warhorse, Bucephalus ('Ox-head'). Alexander was about 13 when he first acquired the horse (c. 343 BCE) and he rode Bucephalus throughout his major campaigns until the horse's death following the Battle of the Hydaspes (326 BCE).

them about the Persian military and the condition of the roads that led to the empire's interior (Plutarch, *Life of Alexander* 4–5). Arrian tells us that, from an early age, he enjoyed a formidable entourage of friends and hangers-on, all of whom stood in awe of him (1.14.4). He was a naturally gifted horseman. As a boy of barely 13, his equestrian skills perhaps outstripped even those of his father and his grooms, a fact illustrated by the dramatic story of how he acquired the horse that he would ride all the way from Macedon to India, the indefatigable Bucephalus.

A Thessalian horse trader, Philoneicus, had paraded the pedigreed stallion before Philip, asking a sum of 13 talents (an enormous sum in the fourth century BCE that likely would have been enough to offer the average person a living wage for an entire lifetime). Although Philip and his grooms tried to mount the animal, they failed miserably. The seemingly uncontrollable horse thwarted them all in turn. Thereafter, Philip's response to the animal was disgust. Alexander's was fascination. And, as Philip rebuked Philoneicus and demanded that he take the horse away, Alexander pleaded with his father, arguing that he was losing a most excellent horse. For, according to Alexander, the problem was not the horse at all, but the lack of skill and courage with which they had attempted to mount him. Philip chafed at his son's apparent insolence and, effectively, dared him to do better. He did. And he

Right: The teenaged Alexander and Bucephalus, as imagined by a nineteenth-century magazine illustrator.

The Breaking of Bucephalus

Once, Philoneicus the Thessalian brought Bucephalus, offering to sell him to Philip for 13 talents, and they went down into the plain to try the horse, who appeared to be savage and altogether intractable, neither allowing any one to mount him, nor heeding the voice of any of Philip's attendants, but rearing up against all of them. Then Philip was perturbed and ordered the horse to be led away, believing him to be altogether wild and unbreakable; but Alexander, who was nearby, said: 'What a horse they are losing, because, for lack of skill and courage, they cannot manage him!' At first, Philip held his peace; but, as Alexander would not be silent and showed great distress, he said: 'Do you find fault with your elders? Do you believe that you know more than they do or are better able to manage a horse than them?' 'This horse, at any rate,' said Alexander, 'I could manage better.' 'And if you should not, what penalty will you pay for your rashness?' 'Indeed,' said Alexander, 'I will pay you the entire price of the horse.' There was laughter at this, and then an agreement between father and son as to the forfeiture, and, at once, Alexander ran to the horse, took hold of his reins, and turned him toward the sun; for he had noticed, as it would seem, that the horse was greatly disturbed by the sight of his own shadow falling in front of him and dancing about. And after he had calmed the horse a little in this way, and had stroked him with his hand, when he saw that he was full of spirit and courage, he quietly cast aside his mantle and with a light spring safely bestrode him. Then, with a little pressure of the reins on the bit, and without striking him or tearing his mouth, he held him in hand; but when he saw that the horse was rid of the fear that had beset him, and was impatient for the course, he gave him his head, and at last urged him on with sterner tone and thrust of foot. Philip and his company were speechless with anxiety at first; but when Alexander made the turn in proper fashion and came back to them proud and exultant, all the rest broke into loud cries, but his father, as we are told, actually shed tears of joy, and when Alexander had dismounted, kissed him, saying: 'My son, seek for yourself a kingdom equal to you; Macedonia is not big enough.'

(Plutarch, *Life of Alexander* 6)

Above: 'Alexander taming Bucephalus', Sodoma, fresco (c. 1516), Agostino Chigi's wedding chamber, Villa Farnesina, Rome.

Right: Fourteenth-century manuscript illustration from *Historia de Preliis Alexandri Magni* ('History of the Battles of Alexander the Great'): Philip entrusting young Alexander the Great to Aristotle.

did so by a demonstration of his keen observational skills and, rare for Alexander, a display of marked gentleness toward the animal. For his impressive showing, Philip bought the horse and made a gift of the sturdy black stallion with the white blaze on his forehead to his son. The name Alexander chose for him means 'Ox-head' and one imagines it could have been as readily applied to the stubborn young prince himself.

The Pupil of Aristotle

But Alexander gravitated toward more intellectual and artistic pursuits as well. He was an avid lover of poetry and drama. He is said to have slept with a copy of Homer's *Iliad* under his pillow and to have known the works of Euripides by heart. Appropriate then that, when Philip sought out an academic mentor for his son, he tapped the most celebrated philosopher of the day, Aristotle (384–322 BCE), whom he welcomed to court at Macedon and set up in his own school in the Precinct of the Nymphs at Mieza on the slopes of Mt. Vermion. In this rural, idyllic setting, some distance away from the raucous drinking parties, sexual escapades and political intrigues of the Macedonian capital at Pella, Alexander would be trained in politics, philosophy and science by one of the Greek world's most dexterous minds.

The eccentric Aristotle was hardly your ordinary philosopher. He dressed in dandified extravagance and curled his thinning hair. Glistening rings graced several of his fingers. He spoke with a slight lisp and moved with a certain affect that, together with his gaudy wardrobe, must have given him the feel of a Greek Liberace. After studying for 20 years at Plato's Academy, his master had snubbed him, choosing his nephew Speusippus to succeed him as head of Athens' famed philosophical school instead. Thereafter, Aristotle struck out on his own, travelling to Asia Minor with Xenocrates, another of Plato's pupils, and making a name for himself in the court of Hermias, the tyrant of Atarneus, in the region of Greek Aeolis in Asia Minor. There, Aristotle founded his first school and took his first wife, Pythias, the much-coveted daughter of the tyrant. He also acted as a diplomatic middle man between Hermias and Philip of Macedon, who was trying to secure allies in Asia Minor, no doubt in preparation for a planned invasion.

Impressed with this flashy philosopher-statesman, Philip soon invited him to head up his own Royal Academy at Macedon. Philip handpicked classmates to matriculate with his son in the school of Aristotle, a retinue of young Macedonian nobles, many of whom came to play critical roles in Alexander's life and campaigns. They were his lifelong friend and lover, Hephaestion, Cassander, son of Antipater, one of Philip's top generals, Ptolemy, son of Lagus, the future master of Egypt, Harpalus, later Alexander's Royal Treasurer, and Marsyas of Pella, who later commemorated those heady days at Mieza in

Right: Nineteenth-century magazine illustration showing Aristotle and his pupil, Alexander.

his unfortunately lost *The Education of Alexander.* At least one Greek appears to have been part of the class as well, Nearchus the Cretan, who not only came to command Alexander's fleet, but wrote a history of Alexander, elements of which have come down to us through the influence of Cleitarchus, although some scholars believe that Arrian may have had Nearchus' work itself at his disposal. Obviously, the group forged powerful bonds in their time together at Mieza. Their lives remained intimately linked from that moment forward.

Alexander Takes the Field: First Forays into Battle

By 340 BCE, Philip had faith enough in his then 16-year-old son to leave him at Pella as regent while he campaigned against Perinthus and Byzantium. Philip left behind his trusted general, Antipater, at the capital for good measure as well, perhaps to act in an advisory capacity should some crisis arise.

When it did, Alexander quickly proved his mettle. The troublesome Madoi from Thrace on Macedon's eastern border had revolted – that was Alexander's story at least. The young prince sprang into action and launched a campaign to quash the would-be uprising. Commanding troops on the battlefield for the first time, he easily defeated his opponents. He went on to take their capital city and to rename it, not for his father the king, who already had namesake cities at Philippi and Philippopolus, but for himself. Alexandropolis was Alexander's first civic foundation, the first of many.

While Alexander was leading his first campaign, Philip was laying siege to the important cities of Perinthus and Byzantium on the Bosporus, near the Black Sea. Philip's excursions into Asia Minor sought to take advantage of an Achaemenid Persia in disarray. If he could command the two cities that guarded the critical trade route from the Black Sea to the Sea of Marmara and, beyond, via the Dardanelles, to the Aegean, Philip would control the flow of supplies to Persia and Greece and the gateway between the Balkans and the East. Although their empire was still wealthy and stable in the heartland, the Great Kings of Persia had an increasingly difficult time maintaining and controlling their outlying possessions.

Revolts in the earlier fourth century BCE had bedevilled Persia's western governors (satraps) and, when precious but troublesome Egypt had joined in the proceedings, the empire nearly imploded. The Great King, Artaxerxes III (r. 358–338 BCE), mustering all the resources at his disposal had

Facing page: View of the archaeological remains at Pella, northern Greece, the Macedonian capital under Philip and Alexander.

finally steadied matters, not long before Philip cast his eye eastward. Although Philip had pledged to lead a Panhellenic campaign to avenge the wrongs Persia had committed against the Greeks and to free at last the Greek colonies on the coast of Asia Minor from Persian harassment, the mouthy Athenian orator, Demosthenes, had succeeded in convincing his city that Philip, and not Persia, was the real threat to Athenian liberty.

As it turns out, led by the Athenians, Philip's erstwhile Greek allies cut a deal with the Great King and helped to thwart the Macedonian king's sieges on the Bosporus, one of the very few military failures of Philip's career. Harassed relentlessly by Athenian marines, Philip barely extricated his fleet from the Black Sea. To add injury to insult, his land forces were attacked on the way home by the primitive but vicious Triballi people. In the fighting, Philip suffered a severe thigh wound that left him permanently lame thereafter.

Returning home to Pella in 339 BCE, Philip must have felt the profound sting of his sudden reversal of fortune. The promising hope of leading a coalition of Macedonians and Greeks against Achaemenid Persia had turned in on itself as the majority of the Greek city-states, including Athens, Thebes and Sparta, now sided with the Persia against *him*. Philip would have to win a decisive victory to turn back the tide. The stage was set for Chaeronea.

Above: Philip of Macedon (far right) loses an eye to an arrow at the siege of Methone.

Battle of Chaeronea

Philip's first move was a diplomatic ruse whereby he sent ambassadors to Athens and Thebes, no doubt with instructions to play one against the other in an attempt to capitalize on the two city-states' long-held suspicions of one another. Philip seemed particularly keen to come to an accord with Athens, but Demosthenes continued to employ his considerable oratorical skill to paint Philip as a power-hungry devil bent on dominating the whole of Greece. Philip had seen first-hand the power of even a fraction of the Athenian navy on the Bosporus, and he knew that, either by alliance or military defeat, he would have to bring the Athenians to heel before a full-blown invasion of Asia would be possible.

Philip marched south with only his southern neighbours, the Thessalians, as allies. At his side was his son, Alexander, whom he would grant a significant role in the battle that loomed. By September, the terror-struck Athenian assembly had received word of Philip's coming. The Macedonian king had occupied Elatea, a key way-station on the main road to central Greece, and to Thebes and Athens. The Greek allies, led by Athens and Thebes, moved to establish a line of defence at Chaeronea near the Cephisus River. The armies met at dawn in August 338 BCE, their numbers roughly even. The Greeks fielded some 35,000 infantry and 2000 cavalry. Philip mustered about 30,000 infantry and 2000 cavalry. The Greeks' right wing was led by Thebes' celebrated Sacred Band, with 10,000 Athenian hoplites stationed on the left. The Greek centre was comprised of a hodgepodge of the remaining allies from Achaea, Megara, Chalcis, Corinth, Epidaurus and a smattering of hired mercenaries.

Philip's primary concern was the well-disciplined Sacred Band that had broken the Spartan lines at Leuctra in 371 BCE. The Athenians on the left, although masters of the sea, did not possess the same prowess on land. These were citizen-

Below: Athenian orator Demosthenes (384–322 BCE) speaks out against Philip and Macedonian expansion.

Facing page: An artist's rendering of the Battle of Chaeronea, which resulted in a resounding victory for Philip and Macedon and made the Macedonian king the effective leader of Greece (with the exception of Sparta).

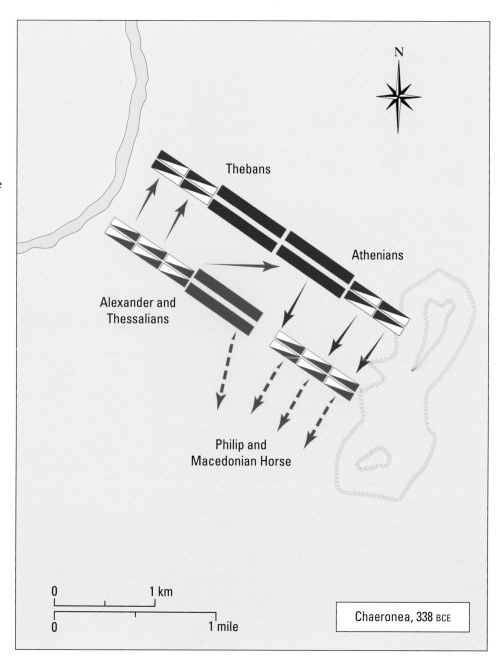

soldiers, who could not boast the same training
and resolve as Thebes' elite infantrymen and had
showed a tendency to become disorganized at
the slightest sign of trouble. Philip then displayed
supreme confidence in the 18-year-old Alexander
by placing him in charge of the left flank that
would confront the Sacred Band. It was Theban
discipline that sealed the fate of the Greek allies that
day, for when Philip joined battle, commanding
the Macedonian right, he slightly outflanked the
Athenians, but in doing so he had crafted a cunning
trap. The Macedonian centre and left had held
back, gently but significantly, refusing battle. The
Athenians, mistakenly thinking that Macedonian
communications had faltered, drifted further left
and launched an impassioned, if disorderly, assault
against Philip's lines. As Philip had anticipated, the
Sacred Band held firm, creating a gap in the allied
lines, into which rode Alexander. With the Greek
lines broken and the Sacred Band isolated, the
Macedonians had effectively dealt the death blow
and Philip had achieved the decisive victory that he
so desperately needed.

Rift between Father and Son

After attending the Congress of Corinth in 337 BCE
and solidifying his position as *hegemon* ('leader') of
Greece and commander of a Panhellenic campaign
against Persia, the always-libidinous Philip returned

home and began a torrid affair with Cleopatra, a true Macedonian noblewoman and the niece of one of his generals, Attalus. Soon thereafter, Philip made Cleopatra his lawful wife. This new marriage did not sit well with Alexander's mother, Olympias, for whom it represented at least a stinging insult, or, more dangerously, a flat repudiation. Although Macedonians were generally comfortable with polygamy, Olympias had a son and potential heir to consider, not to mention her own standing and influence at court, which she believed to be directly threatened by Philip's new marriage.

At the wedding feast, tensions escalated when, during his toast, Attalus wished Philip the good fortune of having a true-born *Macedonian* heir. Macedonian weddings were typically followed by heavy drinking among both celebrants and guests, but Attalus' toast can hardly be written off as a mere drunken rant. The general's clear implication, of course, was that, because Alexander's mother hailed from Epirus and not Macedon, the crown prince was in fact a half-breed, unworthy to wear the Macedonian crown. Alexander was rightly livid and may have killed Attalus, had not Philip drawn his sword to put an end to the quarrel. Alexander demurred, but it was a slur that he would not forget.

Olympias left court for her home in Epirus and Alexander followed, for a time, a fact that suggests that tensions between father and son were, initially

at least, very real. Thereafter, Alexander travelled to Illyria; history does not record his reasons for doing so, although, here again, we would be on solid ground in concluding that Alexander felt some sense of alienation from his father. Would he have gone so far as to consider, even briefly, an alliance with the Illyrians against Philip? It is impossible to say, although not beyond the realm of possibility for the headstrong Alexander. He would have been a mere pretender to the throne with Philip still living and his chances of outfighting his battle-hardened father and his corps of seasoned generals would likely have been slim, but the young man had been shamed publicly at court and his rage may have driven him to contemplate a foolhardy coup. The question of whether Alexander's succession was ever in doubt in Philip's mind, even after Cleopatra was with child, is another matter altogether.

Philip was too smart, too calculating to consider passing over the gifted and charismatic Alexander, who had already proven himself in battle both with and without his father at his side. The young man who gamely commanded the Macedonian left against Thebes' dreaded Sacred Band at Chaeronea – whose battlefield skills may have been the primary cause of Macedon's sweeping victory – was a source of pride to his father and the obvious choice to inherit the throne. Philip no doubt had cringed at Attalus' ill-advised toast and only intervened at the prospect that his son and his general were likely to do mortal harm to one another. He may have lost interest in Olympias' bed, but he would have been a fool to turn his back on the talented Alexander,

regardless of his son's occasional insolence. And Philip was no fool.

One last rift arose between them when the Persian satrap of Caria, Pixodarus, attempted to contract a marriage alliance between his house and Philip's. Philip, who shrank at the prospect of hitching his heir to a Persian vassal, offered the mentally-deficient Philip Arrhidaeus instead. Feeling slighted once again, Alexander interfered and went to Pixodarus offering himself in his half-brother's place, a move that served to sabotage the marriage and infuriate Philip, who had Alexander hauled back to court to be formally reprimanded, but not before sending Attalus to Asia Minor on a scouting expedition, thereby obviating the possibility of another brawl between them. Philip chastised Alexander for meddling and explained the rationale for his decision in no uncertain terms: Alexander was too good to become the son-in-law of a barbarian king.

Philip did not banish his son from the kingdom for the affront, the punishment he inflicted on Alexander's friends Harpalus, Nearchus and Ptolemy, who Philip was convinced had goaded the

Above: Coin of Alexander of Epirus, king of the Molossians (r. 350–331 BCE), brother of Olympias and uncle of Alexander, probably depicting the head of Zeus.

prince into his recent bad behaviour. That Philip wanted to keep Alexander close again suggests that he was grooming him for the succession. The fact that Philip made overtures to his estranged wife, Olympias, with a proposal to marry their daughter to her brother, Alexander, king of the Molossians, further confirms that the Macedonian king was taking firm steps to ameliorate the concerns of both Alexander and his mother about their roles in the future of Macedon. The marriage of Philip and Olympias' daughter to the slighted queen's brother would help to heal the rift between the members of the royal family.

The Murder of Philip

In October 336 BCE Philip decided to hold a grand state wedding complete with games at Macedon's old ceremonial capital of Aegae. He invited dignitaries from around the Greek world to attend. It was as if, before launching his long-desired and imminent campaign against Persia, Philip sought to put an end, once and for all, to any lingering concerns about his relationship to Alexander and Olympias. The Macedonian king now understood that the two were a kind of package deal. Alexander remained close to his mother and, whatever had passed between Philip and Olympias, the king knew that he had to make nice with the mother of his heir or face the possibility of rebellion by him. If, in fact, as some scholars think, Philip planned to leave Alexander behind as regent as he led his forces into Asia Minor, he needed to be certain of his son's loyalty. The wedding gala went off without

a hitch. Even the Athenians showed up, carrying gold crowns that they presented to the Macedonian king. The following day, however, as the sun rose and the games were set to commence, Philip entered the theatre between two Alexanders, one his son, the other now his son-in-law. He had ordered the members of his royal bodyguard to keep their distance. He wished to demonstrate to all the Greeks in attendance that he hardly needed armed men to protect him anymore, so much power and goodwill had he acquired. He was gravely mistaken. A young nobleman from that very bodyguard, Pausanias of Orestis, drew a short sword from beneath his cloak, lunged at Philip and stabbed him through the ribs, burying his blade in the king up to its hilt. Philip fell and died instantly. The assassin attempted to run, but tripped on a protruding root, to be shortly thereafter run through with javelins.

Pausanias was no conspirator, but a loner with a grudge. Philip had detractors, enemies, surely. But few, if any, would have dared so brazen an action; they simply had too much to lose. This attack was personal. Pausanias was a former lover of Philip's, whom the king had discarded in favour of another. Pausanias had bristled at the slight and made a scene at court. Philip brushed Pausanias' antics aside. Attalus, however, who seems to have possessed a nasty habit of inserting himself, unwelcomed, into already tense situations, decided to teach young Pausanias a lesson on his king's behalf. In an episode that illustrates the sheer brutality of Macedonian court life, Attalus invited Pausanias to a dinner party at his home and filled him with wine until

the inebriated youth could scarcely stand. He and his friends then gang-raped pitiful Pausanias as the other guests cheered them on. As if that was not enough, Attalus, thereafter, handed the young man over to his grooms, who beat him up and left him for dead in a stall alongside the mules. Pausanias recovered and went to Philip, demanding some recompense. He received none. The bald fact of the matter was that Philip needed Attalus, the general, far more than his former plaything. Philip of Macedon died because of a jilted lover and the very bad behaviour of the same general who almost cost him his relationship with his son. If Philip's assassin had accomplices in the strictest sense, they were probably loyal friends, aggrieved at the shame Pausanias had endured and angered by their king's utter failure to address it. Philip's dream of invading the great Achaemenid Persian Empire as leader of an allied Greek world, died on the floor of the theatre at Aegae. But a new dream was born there as well, a dream that likely stretched beyond anything that Philip ever considered. For the man who would now rule Macedon did not play by traditional rules. He did not accept typical boundaries. There is no compelling reason to suspect that Alexander played any role at all in his father's assassination, but there is no doubt also that he benefitted significantly from the timing of it. The invasion of Asia was now his and it was his to seek a kingdom equal to his limitless imagination.

Facing page: Assassination of Philip at Aegae by a member of his bodyguard, Pausanias of Orestis.

King Alexander III: The Journey Begins

Before Alexander could consider an invasion of the Persian Empire, he had to resolve troubles much closer to home. Surrounded by potential threats, the young king would be forced, at the very outset of his reign, to prove himself his father's equal.

Almost immediately upon Philip's death, Antipater scooped up Alexander and presented him before the Macedonian army, which at once acclaimed him king. Intimates of Alexander, Perdiccas, Leonnatus and Attalus, son of Adromenes, had swiftly cornered and killed the assassin Pausanias, a fact that has led some scholars to suggest that Alexander and Olympias engineered Philip's murder and that Alexander enlisted the help of these three close friends to ensure that Pausanias would never speak a word of the plot. Rumours certainly circulated regarding Olympias. Justin (IX.7) preserves a story that, on the very night of her return from exile, Alexander's mother placed a crown on Pausanias' corpse and erected a tumulus in his memory. Nevertheless, the alacrity with which the army acclaimed Alexander and the support of Philip's seemingly loyal general, Antipater, argues strongly against Alexander's complicity in Philip's assassination or even that anyone but a very few had suspicion of it. The fact did not stop Macedon's most vocal foil, the Athenian Demosthenes, from sending secret communications to the remaining two members of Philip's top triad of generals,

Facing page: Alexander before the tomb of Achilles (his 'ancestor'), by Giovanni Paolo Pannini. Alexander was a great lover of Homer and was said to have slept with a copy of the *Iliad* under his pillow.

Right: A bust of Athenian statesman, orator and vocal opponent of Macedon, Demosthenes (384–322 BCE).

Right: Map of the expansion of Macedon from 359–336 BCE, under Philip and Alexander. When the Macedonian king became *hegemon* ('leader') of the League of Corinth (here in blue), the Macedonians effectively controlled all of Greece (with the exception of Sparta).

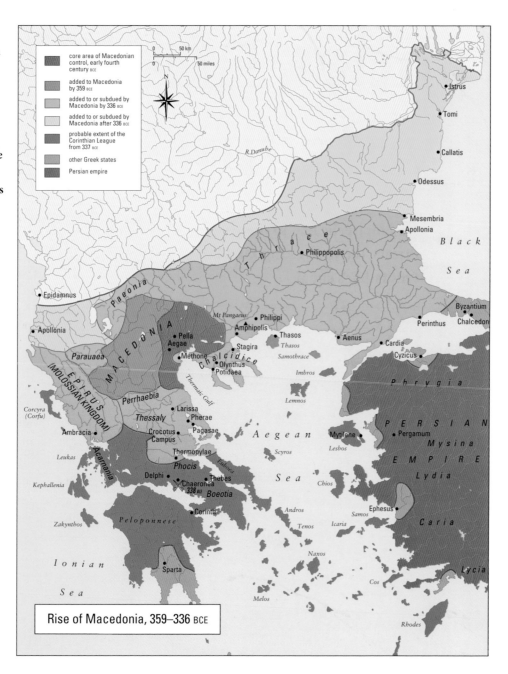

Rise of Macedonia, 359–336 BCE

Attalus and Parmenion, both of whom were in Asia Minor. Demosthenes, at least, hoped to convince them that Alexander, whom he called a 'mere booby', had spearheaded the coup against his father. Demosthenes had offered Parmenion and Attalus full Athenian support if they chose to act against Alexander. But he had also hedged his bets by making overtures to Darius III, the Great King of Persia, asking for Persian resources to support an Athenian-led revolt against Macedon. The Great King was unimpressed. He wrote back to Demosthenes in response, 'I will not give you gold; stop asking me for it; you will not get it' (Aeschines, *In Ctesiphon* 238; cf. Diodorus Siculus, XVII.7.12). Aristotle and Diodorus suggest that Demosthenes' communications with Attalus actually predated Philip's death, and that the troublemaking general himself may have played a significant role in Philip's assassination. The problem with the theory is that this would have required Pausanias to be in league with the same man who engineered his brutal gang rape, the very event that led to the future assassin's falling out with Philip.

Danger on All Sides

Meanwhile, the Triballians, the tribe that had fallen upon Philip during his retreat from Byzantium, were fomenting rebellion in Thrace. And in Illyria, Cleitus, the son of Bardylis (the king who had killed Philip's predecessor Perdiccas III in battle), was raising his own challenge to Macedonian hegemony in the region. Alexander now faced the potential of resistance on multiple fronts: the Greeks to the

Left: 'Alexander and Diogenes', by Sebastiano Ricci (circa 1700). While at Corinth, Alexander made a point of visiting Diogenes the Cynic, who was living in a wooden tub on the city's outskirts.

him alive to Macedon, and, if that was not possible, to kill him with the greatest haste. Parmenion was duly convinced and Attalus duly executed. Back in Macedon, others, like the Lyncestian brothers, Arrhabaeus and Heromenes, were arrested and executed as well, either based on some connection to the assassination or even some connection to Attalus. Perhaps significantly, a third brother, Alexander the Lyncestian, was first to pay homage to Alexander as king upon Philip's death. Thereafter, the Lyncestian became an important cavalry commander in Alexander's army.

Alexander and Diogenes

Having dealt with the Asian high command as well as conspirators and antagonists on the home front, Alexander marched south to claim formally his position as *hegemon* of the League of Corinth, the position that had been conferred upon his father by a congress of collective Greeks in the wake of Chaeronea. While there, Alexander learned that the celebrated philosopher and self-proclaimed 'citizen of the world' (*kosmopolites*), Diogenes of Sinope (c. 404–323 BCE), was living in a wooden tub on the outskirts of the city. Diogenes had earned the nickname 'the Dog' (*kunos*) based on his belief that all natural functions, including masturbation, copulation, urination and defecation,

south led by Athens, the Thracians to the east, the Illyrians to the west; and from within, at least two of his father's trusted generals, one of whom, Attalus, had never been impressed with the upstart, half-Epirote Macedonian prince, and who now also had a personal stake in Alexander's potential undoing, since his niece, Cleopatra, had given birth to a child, and both she and the newborn would likely be

doomed if Alexander remained in power. As would become his custom, Alexander acted quickly and boldly. He sent a trusted friend, Hecataeus, with a small hand-picked force to Parmenion's Asian headquarters. His orders were simple. He was to convince Parmenion that Alexander valued him and still wished him to be an integral part of the Asian campaign. As for Attalus, Hecataeus was to return

could and should be performed in public, as a dog performs them. Alexander located the founder of the Cynic movement sunbathing naked beside his tub. Impressed at Diogenes' brazen reputation, the young Macedonian king offered him anything he desired. Diogenes asked the most powerful man in the Greek world merely to stand aside and stop blocking his sun. Alexander's men jeered at the pretentious philosopher and hurled curses at him for his insolence before the king, but Alexander, fascinated all the more, raised a hand and stopped them cold, exclaiming, 'If I were not Alexander,

I would be Diogenes.' To which Diogenes is said to have responded, 'If I were not Diogenes, I would be Diogenes also' (Arrian VII.2.1; Plutarch, *Moralia*, 331; Diogenes Laertius VI.32, 38, 60 and 68). From that day forward, Alexander seems to have maintained a healthy respect for Diogenes and his movement. 'The Dog's' pupil, Onesicritus, would later join Alexander's campaign and write a biography of him. Before departing central Greece, Alexander dutifully made a dedication at the Panhellenic oracle at Delphi. He did so as the undisputed master of the Greek world. Back home in the Balkans, however, matters were hardly settled. The Triballians remained a nuisance, which Alexander had to address.

Defeat of the Triballians and Cleitus

Alexander marched into Thrace by way of the Shipka Pass. There he noticed that the Triballian tribesmen had fortified themselves on the hillsides behind wagons, effectively making barricades out of them. But the canny Triballians had a more ingenious use of the wagons in mind than mere protection. As Alexander's men entered the pass, the tribesmen began rolling the wagons down the hillsides, hoping to crush the Macedonians before having to engage in proper combat with them. Thinking on his feet, Alexander ordered his men to make lanes through which the carts could pass and he had his infantry lock into tight formation and place their shields above their heads, so that when the wagons did reach the bottom of the hill, they would either strike nothing, or the closely packed

Below: The Macedonians battle the Triballians (and their carts) in the Shipka Pass (Thrace, modern Bulgaria).

(and therefore protected) ranks of the Macedonian phalanx. Not a single Macedonian was lost in the Triballians' cart attack, and with the carts no longer a threat, Alexander routed the tribesmen. The Triballian king, Syrmus, retreated to an island in the Danube.

Vowing that the Triballians would never again be a thorn in the Macedonians' side, Alexander pursued. He commandeered canoes of local fishermen and ordered his men to cut wood and fill their tents with chaff to make large rafts. With these makeshift rafts, Alexander and 1500 cavalrymen crossed the Danube River, their horses swimming alongside them (some sources suggest that as many as 4000 of Alexander's infantry crossed as well). It was a daring and exceptional feat, the likes of which would become commonplace for Alexander. Instead of going after Syrmus directly, Alexander crossed all the way to the north bank of the river and attacked a settlement of Getae, whose numbers were far superior to Alexander's, in a devastatingly effective display intended to frighten Syrmus into surrender. Even before Alexander could offer sacrifice to Zeus, Heracles and the river god for permitting his crossing, he received overtures from Syrmus. With the capture of the Triballian king, the threat in Thrace was brought to a definitive end. In fact, Syrmus managed to conclude a treaty with Alexander, and the Triballians dutifully sent a contingent of troops for the army that invaded Asia in 334 BCE.

With Alexander away from court and Philip dead, Olympias now enjoyed the freedom to act

against her nemesis, Cleopatra. Returning to court from Epirus, she cruelly engineered the death of Philip's last wife and her infant daughter. We are told that Alexander was horrified by his mother's actions, although apparently he did nothing to protect Cleopatra and her progeny – perhaps his focus lay elsewhere. For, by August of 335, only weeks from his success on the Danube, Alexander was en route by forced marches to face Cleitus in Illyria.

As Alexander approached, Cleitus holed up in the fortified stronghold of Pellium, located in a narrow glen near the river Eordaicus. The Illyrian king hoped to spring a trap on Alexander, for, as the Macedonian began to lay siege to the fortress,

Above: The Shipka Pass today. The 13 km (nine-mile) mountain pass is now part of Bulgaria's Bulgarka Nature Park.

Left: Alexander (foreground) is depicted crossing the Granicus River with his Companion cavalry. He wears a lion's head helmet (a nod to Heracles) and uses a leopard-skin saddle pad (a nod to Dionysus).

Cleitus' Taulantian allies – a neighbouring people recruited to aid the Illyrians in throwing off the yoke of Macedonian control – were arriving with a large levy to block Alexander's escape route, a narrow wooded pass against a sheer cliff with the river beneath.

Learning of the presence of the Taulantians at his rear, Alexander ordered his men to narrow their ranks and line up 120 men deep. They held their 4.8m (16ft) pikes (*sarissas*) upright, moving them in unison in a terrifying show of military discipline. Some 200 cavalrymen perched on the wings of the narrowed phalanx. The Macedonian display alone led some of the Taulantian tribesmen to break ranks and run. Thereafter, Alexander ordered his men to attack. As they did so, the king commanded the Macedonians to raise a war cry and beat their spears against their shields. The Taulantians who remained in position were no doubt alarmed, but they hunkered down and prepared for the impending Macedonian onslaught. Several days of fighting ensued, after which the victorious Macedonians cornered the survivors in the stronghold of Pellium, breaching the fortress's defences with ease and plundering and setting fire to the citadel. Cleitus himself, now utterly discredited, escaped and fled north. Alexander considered following him, but trouble

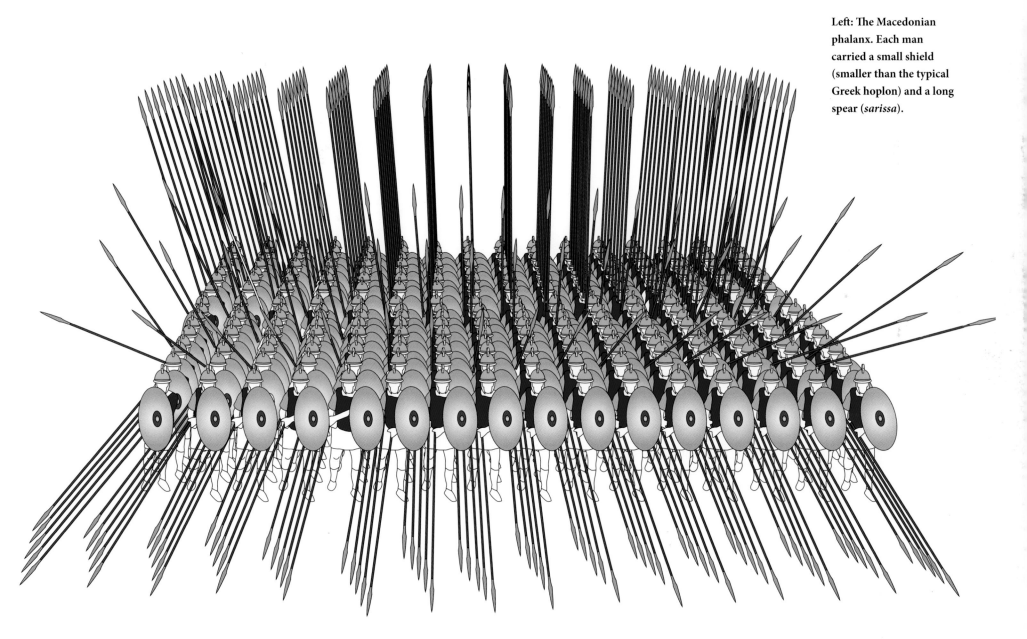

Left: The Macedonian phalanx. Each man carried a small shield (smaller than the typical Greek hoplon) and a long spear (*sarissa*).

among the Greek city-states to the south now commanded his attention.

The Revolt of Thebes

Word arrived that Thebes had revolted, apparently at the news that Alexander had been killed fighting in the far north. One might have expected Demosthenes' Athenians to be the first to strike out against Alexander, but indecisive Athens would never have been quite so bold. The Thebans, however, had gone so far as to assassinate two members of the city's Macedonian garrison and imprison the rest. Less than two weeks removed from the Illyrian campaign, Alexander was on Thebes' doorstep laying siege to the city. Even with the Macedonian king outside the city walls, the Thebans persisted in their belief that Alexander had fallen on the Danube. Surely the man attacking their city was Antipater, or even Alexander the Lyncestian. The Thebans were sorely mistaken.

At first, Alexander demanded only that Thebes surrender the leaders of the rebellion. When they refused to do so, he assumed a much harsher attitude. By October 335 BCE, Thebes belonged to Alexander, 6000 Thebans having been killed and another 3000 taken prisoner. We are told that Alexander referred the fate of the city to a council of Greeks, representatives of the remaining cities of the

Facing page: **Alexander rides through Thebes in 335 BCE, having put down the city's rebellion. Illustration from** *Hutchinson's History of the Nations*, **1915 (litho) by Charles R. Stanton.**

The Fate of Thebes: They Had It Coming

'People felt that Thebes, at long last, had been punished for her treachery – she had paid the penalty for her betrayal of Greece in the Persian War, her capture of Plataea during the truce, the merciless enslavement of its population and the massacre, for which she alone was responsible, of men who had surrendered not to her, but to Sparta, and the devastation of a countryside in which the united armies of Greece had driven back the Persian invader, and, lastly, for the murderous malignancy she showed towards Athens when she voted in favour of the suggestion, put forward by the Lacedaemonian confederacy, that the people of Athens should be sold into slavery. Everyone now declared that the calamity had been preceded by many warning signs from heaven – signs ignored at the moment, but remembered now, long afterwards, and clearly proved by the event to have been prophetic of the coming doom. The allied troops who took part in the fighting were entrusted by Alexander with the final settlement of the fate of Thebes. They decided to garrison the Cadmeia, but to raze the city itself to the ground.' (Arrian, I.9) [The 'allied' troops to which Arrian refers are Macedon's allies from the League of Corinth and comprised the council to which Alexander supposedly referred Thebes' fate.]

League of Corinth, but this may simply be the report of apologetic sources attempting to let Alexander off the hook for what happened next. For his part, Arrian, probably based on Ptolemy's account, goes to some length to demonstrate that the Thebans deserved the punishment inflicted upon them.

The decision was that Thebes should be razed to the ground. Alexander spared only the house of the illustrious poet, Pindar. Here again, as he would for so much of his life, the king evinced his deep appreciation for the great poets of Greece. But one of Greece's great cities, one of the triad that, along with Athens and Sparta, had for more than 150 years contended for domination of the Greek world, had been annihilated utterly. With potential enemies in

Thrace, Illyria and mainland Greece eliminated or subdued, Alexander now readied himself for the great invasion his father had envisioned, although the vision of Alexander would be far more sweeping.

Securing Macedon

Back in Macedon, Alexander received the suggestion from both Antipater and Parmenion that, before invading Asia, he should marry one of their daughters and father a child. Perhaps not wishing to convey such prestige on one general at the expense of the other, Alexander declined both offers. Antipater, who was now about 60, was tasked with remaining in Macedon and was imbued with full authority to supervise Greece

Above: Alexander and Timoclea at Thebes. Although Timoclea was said to have killed one of Alexander's Thracian captains (in response to having been raped), she gained pardon from Alexander for her dignity and boldness when she proudly reported to him that her brother had fought against the Macedonians at Chaeronea for the 'liberty of the Greeks' (c. 1615, by Domenichino, 1581–1641, oil on canvas).

men had played under his father's command. In addition, individuals loyal to Parmenion played significant roles in the hierarchy of the Macedonian army. One of the old general's sons, Philotas, was commander of the Companion cavalry, another commanded the shield bearers, and three other infantry commanders were Parmenion's close friends. Further, if Alexander had the slightest suspicion that Parmenion had been conspiring with Attalus after Philip's assassination, he knew it would be better to keep him close than to leave him in Greece with even the remotest possibility that Athens or Sparta could persuade him to turn against his king. Antipater, at least, had proven that he could be trusted from half a world away.

Before departing from Macedon, Alexander lavished gifts, lands and monies upon his fellow Macedonian nobles and allies in the Balkans, Epirus and Greece. He was no doubt buying their continued loyalty and support, especially close to home, where many Macedonian aristocrats had tried to dissuade him from invading Asia. They were convinced that the best course of action was to remain in Macedon, for now, to solidify his hold over Greece and the Balkans and to ensure that recent troubles would not rear their heads again. But Alexander would not be deterred. Amazed at the small fortune that Alexander had handed out, especially at a time when the Macedonian treasury had been heavily depleted by Philip's military upgrades and campaigns, the king's close friend, Perdiccas, asked, 'What are you leaving yourself?' Alexander responded, 'My hopes.' 'Very well, then,'

and the Balkans. Crusty, old Parmenion, who was now nearly 65, would serve as Alexander's deputy commander in the invasion. It is interesting that Alexander chose Parmenion over Antipater to serve as his right hand. Antipater, after all, had ensured his immediate and uncontested acclamation in the wake of his father's death. Perhaps Alexander wished to maintain continuity in the roles the two

replied Perdiccas, 'we who serve with you will share those also' (Plutarch, *Life of Alexander* 15).

It has been suggested that Perdiccas' response may imply that Alexander's Companions were, in fact, helping to bankroll recent and future campaigns, because royal finances were in a sorry state and Alexander was employing most of what remained in the treasury to guarantee allegiances while he travelled abroad. Whatever the case may be, it is clear that those marshals closest to Alexander were ready and willing to place their faith, their lives, and perhaps their fortunes in the care of their king.

Logistics of the Macedonian Army

The army that Alexander would lead into Asia was comprised (including the advance force) of some 43,000 infantry and 6000 cavalry. These numbers are generally agreed upon by Plutarch, Diodorus, Arrian and Polybius. With mercenaries, engineers, slaves and other personnel included, the invading force probably numbered around 65,000. They would have required at least 6000 cavalry horses, perhaps with another 100 or so in reserve, and around 2500 pack animals carrying baggage and provisions. It has been estimated that the grain required to feed both men and animals in the Macedonian invasion force would have exceeded 127,000kg (over 280,000lbs). The water requirement, too, for an army on the move, burning a significant number of calories and often risking dehydration in the process, would have been enormous. In practical application, the army and its pack animals could only carry a 10-day ration

Left: Philotas, the son of Parmenion, Alexander's first commander of the Companion cavalry.

Facing page: The solid body of infantrymen, armed with long spears and shields, was known as a phalanx among the Greeks, and was perfected by Alexander. He divided the phalanx into separate blocks, supported by groups of lightly-armed, skirmishing troops, bowmen and slingers.

of food and water before having to be resupplied, by means of either movable supply trains and transport ships or imposing upon indigenous peoples, settlements and cities along the campaign route.

Although Alexander's force was the size of a significant city in the fourth century BCE, Philip's military reforms had made the Macedonian army lighter and more mobile. No doubt Philip had the prospect and potential problems of an invasion of Asia in mind when he set about overhauling the Macedonian military. For example, Philip had forbade the use of carts on campaign, a move which likely increased the number of baggage animals, but reduced delays that cumbersome wheeled vehicles could produce, especially over rocky or muddy terrain. It has also been suggested that Philip understood the inefficiency of the throat and girth harness employed on pack horses and mules in antiquity. Because the harness was placed directly over the animal's windpipe, the harder the animal strained against the apparatus, the more he cut off his own air supply, meaning the animal was able to pull less weight than he would with a breast or shoulder harness, neither of which had yet reached the Greek world.

Philip had also stripped down much of the protective hoplite infantry armour common to the Greeks, probably dispensing with the breastplate and, quite significantly, the large convex shield, or *hoplon*, which had revolutionized infantry fighting in the seventh century BCE. The *hoplon* was exchanged for a smaller shield and a much longer spear or pike, called the *sarissa*, generally believed to have been 4.8–5.5m (16–18ft) long. The *sarissa* made the Macedonian hoplite phalanx virtually impervious to the new cavalry warfare that had swept across Greece and Asia Minor, devastating the traditional hoplite phalanx and leading to the rise of Thebes, under the command of the innovative cavalry commander and one-time tutor of Philip, Epaminondas.

Despite these reforms, which made the Macedonian infantry formidable, it was Alexander's cavalry that often delivered the death

Right: A Companion cavalryman. The Companions were more heavily-armoured (with breast plates) and carried shorter spears than the members of the Macedonian phalanx. In the interest of increased mobility, the Companions probably carried no shield. The heavier armour is suggestive of the integral role the Macedonian cavalry played in battle.

Right: A sixteenth-century wood carving depicts Alexander the Great on horseback with his army. Alexander looks much the part of a medieval (and not ancient) king and the cavalry carry historically-inaccurate shields, but the artist does depict the Macedonians with their famous *sarissas*.

Facing page: The fleet of Alexander. From a fifteenth-century French manuscript from Curtius' *The History of Alexander the Great*.

blow in his battles. The elite among them, the so-called 'Companions' (*hetairoi*), were effectively a kind of royal bodyguard. Although the Companions had a commander, their true commander was Alexander himself, who rode at the apex of the flying wedge formation borrowed from Thebes, but modified by the Macedonians to devastating effect. The Macedonians might be said to have possessed the world's first true 'shock' cavalry, although certain of its tactics surely originated in Thebes. The whole of Alexander's major cavalry corps carried a smaller version of the infantry *sarissa*, wore body armour and helmets, but probably carried no shield at all. They were built for speed and prepared for direct contact with the enemy. Their body armour, compared with the phalangites' lack of a breast plate, suggests that the Macedonian cavalry was designed to deliver the hammer blow against an opposing force. The phalanx was the anvil.

Crossing to Asia

When Alexander crossed the Hellespont into Asia, he also had as few as 60 or as many as 160 warships at his disposal, perhaps the discrepancy within

ALEXANDRI MAGNI SITIS

the sources has to do with a confusion of what constitutes a warship versus a supply or transport galley. The number 160 may include warships *and* supply ships. Whatever the number was, it would have been dwarfed by the massive Persian fleet, probably comprised of upwards of 400 ships. In short, Persia controlled the sea, a reality to which Alexander paid close heed when formulating his plan of campaign. One is forced to wonder why Darius III allowed Alexander to cross the Hellespont unchallenged and to join the advance force of Parmenion at Abydos on the Asian side of the narrowest point of the Dardanelles.

There are only two logical explanations for why the Great King would allow Alexander to touch Asian soil unimpeded. First, his attention was occupied with a revolt in Egypt; second, Darius III did not recognize Alexander as a threat to Persian supremacy. But when Alexander leapt onto the ground of Asia, hurling his spear into the earth as he did so, his intention was clear. Asia would be battle-won territory. Alexander was bent on making the lands formerly dominated by the Achaemenid kings his own and Darius III had sorely underestimated the young Macedonian's resolve.

Arrived in Asia, Alexander first went to Troy, where he made sacrifice to Athena and poured libations to the heroes of the Greek armies that fought there. He then made a gift of his own armour to the local temple and took in exchange some

Facing page: Achilles (in his chariot) leads funeral games in honour of the fallen Patroclus, by Antoine Vernet (c.1790).

weapons that were said to have been preserved from the Trojan War. He stripped himself and his dear friend, Hephaestion, naked and, smeared with oil, they raced nude to the tombs of Achilles and Patroclus, which they crowned with ceremonial wreaths. Upon laying his wreath at Achilles' tomb, Alexander proclaimed him a 'most fortunate' man, in that he had Homer to celebrate his deeds and preserve his memory. The symbolism of this action would not have been lost on any who witnessed it. A new Achilles had come to Troy, one who, in fact,

Above: The mound of Troy (Hisarlik, northwestern Anatolia). The acropolis walls (pictured here) belong to Troy's layer VII, which is believed to be the site of the Trojan War, fought between a confederation of Greek (Mycenaean) forces and, probably, the inhabitants of a Hittite-controlled trade outpost between 1250–1200 BCE.

believed himself to be descended from the great hero on his mother's side and one who had every intention of seeing the great cities of Asia fall before him as they had to his ancestor.

War with Persia

Memnon of Rhodes, a battle-hardened Greek mercenary and general in the service of the Great King of Persia, was aware of Alexander's money problems and logistical limitations. He wisely advised a scorched-earth policy to repel the Macedonians. He recommended burning the fields and their crops, and even the towns and villages in the vicinity of the Macedonian advance, if necessary.

His strategy may have appeared extreme, but Memnon argued vehemently that these measures would force Alexander to withdraw in short order for lack of provisions. Phase two of Memnon's plan included amassing the Persian army and fleet to invade Macedon while Alexander's army was in retreat and his forces divided. Memnon also pointed out that Alexander led *his* army in person, while Darius did not, a fact that made the Macedonians more impassioned fighters. It was sound advice and it may well have preserved the Great King's empire, at least for a time, but Darius' governors (satraps), especially Arsites of Phrygia, rejected Memnon's advice outright, either because it came from the mouth of a Greek or they still failed to take the threat of Alexander seriously, or they had not yet erased the memory of the last time the Persian armada attempted to invade Greece. The Persians would attempt to thwart Alexander the old-fashioned way. They would face him in pitched battle in the hopes that their numerically superior forces and nearly unlimited financial resources would prevail.

And so on a May afternoon in 334 BCE, the Persian forces took up a position on the plain of Adrasteia, west of the city of Zeleia, where they had held their war council and decided, against Memnon's advice, to stand and fight. The Persian plan was to foil Alexander in the Troad, at the very

Facing page: 'Alexander Mosaic' from House of the Faun, Pompeii, traditionally believed to depict the Battle of Issus. Darius III, the Great King of Persia, is pictured at centre. Roman copy of a Hellenistic painting by Philoxenos of Eretria (late fourth-early third century BCE). Museo Archeologico Nazionale, Naples.

Right: Head from a statue of Asclepius, the Greek god of medicine and healing. Roman copy of a late fifth century BCE original.

The Battle of Salamis

At the decisive Battle of Salamis in 480 BCE, the Athenian admiral Themistocles had defeated a numerically superior Persian fleet, drawing them into the narrow Straits of Salamis, where he used lighter and faster Athenian triremes to ram, board and sink the less manoeuvrable Persian ships, which became ineffective and unmanageable in the tight quarters before the entire fleet could even join the battle.

According to Herodotus, 'the majority of the ships at Salamis were sunk, some destroyed by the Athenians, some by the Aeginetans. Since the Hellenes fought in an orderly fashion by line, but the barbarians were no longer in position and did nothing with forethought, it was likely to turn out as it did' (*Histories* VIII.86).

Below: 'The Battle of Salamis' by Wilhelm von Kaulbach (1804–1874). Maximilianeum, Munich.

gates of Asia, before he could even begin to threaten the Persian interior. The Persians encamped above the plain in an area intersected by the deepest and swiftest section of the River Granicus, which would have been in full swell in late Spring.

The Persians, commanded by Memnon and Arsites, clearly sought to take advantage of their position on the far side of the river. They were numerically superior in cavalry, some 20,000 strong, and, if Alexander dared to cross the river at its deepest point, they were convinced of their ability to ride down from the foothills and crush his forces as they emerged from the river.

The Battle of the Granicus

As Alexander's forces approached the river toward evening, Parmenion advised that the Macedonians encamp for the night. He argued that, because the Macedonian infantry outnumbered the present number of Persian footsoldiers, the Persians would not run the risk of remaining so close through the night but would instead withdraw, increase the numbers of their infantry and prepare to fight again another day. According to Parmenion, any attempt to cross the river under the present circumstances would be a 'grave risk'. The water's depth and the steepness of the banks would present significant obstacles, especially to the Macedonian infantry and would force them to cross in a loose order that would allow the massive Persian cavalry to fall upon the men as they struggled out of the water. In sum, Parmenion pleaded with the king, 'a failure at the outset would be a serious thing now,

and highly detrimental to our success in the long run' (Arrian I.13).

Parmenion was no doubt correct. He had pegged the Persian strategy precisely, and under the average commander his advice would have been well worth heeding, but Alexander was far from average. He rejected Parmenion's counsel and ordered his troops into battle array. He sent Parmenion to take command of the left wing, while he moved to the right. We are told that command of the right, where the Companion cavalry was positioned, already rested with Philotas, Parmenion's son, but

Above: Battle scene of the Macedonian army fighting Persians from the Alexander Sarcophagus, a well-preserved, late fourth-century sarcophagus made of Pentelic marble and adorned with bas-relief carvings showing the campaigns of Alexander (Istanbul Archaeological Museum).

Right: Depiction of Persian warriors, possibly the so-called 'Immortals', from Darius I's palace at Susa. Glazed brick frieze, late sixth century BCE.

Arrian's account suggests that Alexander effectively commanded the right wing himself with Philotas acting as his lieutenant. Beyond Alexander, Philotas and the Companions were the Agrianian spearmen and the archers, both of whom were meant to hold steady and hurl or shoot at the enemy from a distance. Alongside the archers was a composite force of light infantry, a single squadron of the Companion cavalry numbering 200–300 men, and the light skirmishing cavalry (*prodromoi*) usually armed with javelins, although here, because they rode in conjunction with a squadron of the Companions, they carried a cavalry *sarissa* instead of lighter skirmishing weapons. This force was commanded by Amyntas, son of Arrhibaeus, and would be first to cross the Granicus.

On the left, with Parmenion, were stationed the Guard's battalions commanded by another of Parmenion's sons, Nicanor, followed by the heavy infantry battalions commanded by Alexander's close compatriots, Perdiccas and Amyntas, son of Andromenes, one more infantry battalion under Coenus and additional light-armed troops. The allied Thessalian cavalry commanded by Calas, son of Harpalus, held the advance position on the left. The Thessalians were supported by the remaining allied cavalry squadrons of Philip, son of Menelaus, and Agathon. On their immediate right were the remaining infantry battalions, under Craterus and

Meleager, whose position extended all the way to the Macedonian centre.

If the Persians intended to kill Alexander in this first battle, cutting off the serpent's head and putting an end to the Macedonian invasion before it began in earnest, they would have had no problem locating him, for Arrian tells us that he leapt upon his horse before the Macedonian right 'an unmistakable figure in magnificent armour, attended by his suite with an almost ecstatic reverence' (Arrian I.15).

Accounts of what happened next do not agree in certain details. This is especially true of our fullest accounts of the battle (in Arrian and Diodorus). Some scholars have suggested that Alexander's initial rejection of Parmenion's advice was followed by a failed attempt to cross the river, in which the Macedonians took heavy losses and that, thereafter, Alexander resigned himself to camp for the night and try crossing again at dawn. Under this scenario, the actual battle would have taken place the day

Below: 'The Battle of the Granicus' by late-Baroque Italian painter, Francesco Fontebasso (1707–1769); oil on canvas.

after Alexander's arrival at the river and not the very afternoon of it. But Alexander was nothing if not audacious and he proved himself to be a constant risk-taker. Parmenion's cautious admonitions would merely have spurred Alexander on, driven as the young king was to overcome any challenge set in his path. Crossing the Granicus that late May afternoon with the sun in his eyes (as he was riding eastward) against perhaps 20,000 Persian cavalry, who commanded the high ground on the opposite bank may have seemed foolhardy to most, which is precisely why Alexander would have endeavoured to do it. What follows, then, is an educated guess as to how the battle played out, based on sometimes irreconcilable sources.

The Macedonians Advance

The forces of Amyntas, son of Arrhibaeus, were ordered to cross the river first and probably to locate a manageable ford at which to do so. They needed to get across as quickly as possible to minimize their losses and so likely would not have crossed the river in deep water. Amyntas' *prodromoi* were experienced at advance scouting and skirmishing. As such, they were directed to distract and/or engage the numerically superior Persian cavalry on the opposite bank. As Amyntas' troops emerged from the water, they were met with volleys of missiles, which the Persians shot at them continuously from the high ground of the river bank. Despite some losses, the Macedonians gained the river bank and a hand-to-hand struggle ensued. At this point, Alexander, at the head of the right wing, ordered the trumpets to sound and raised the war cry to Ares, the god of battles, advancing into the river himself. Parmenion's forces on the left and the Macedonian heavy infantry followed close behind. With the Persian cavalry brought down from their commanding position and onto the plain, their tactical advantage was eliminated.

As Alexander and the Companion cavalry strode out of the Granicus, the Persians were forced to make a swift and decisive strategic manoeuvre. They spread out their cavalry ranks so as to cover as wide a swath of ground as possible, sending the thickest ranks right at the oncoming Alexander. Memnon and his sons appear to have led the main faction of cavalry

Facing page: Alexander's forces are depicted riding into battle against Memnon, Arsites and the Persians at the Granicus.

squadrons. Their aim was surely to take Alexander out quickly, thereby demoralizing and confusing the Macedonian army, for whom the slightest misstep would have meant being pushed back into the Granicus and to a watery grave. The Persians very nearly regained the upper-hand, for we are told that Alexander and his immediate retinue were thrust post haste into an enemy onslaught. Alexander's cavalry *sarissa* was broken in half in this early fighting, even before a daring charge from the Macedonians' far left by Mithridates, the son-in-law of Darius, the Great King – a canny outflanking manoeuvre that attempted to do in Alexander's forces, while they were already engaged with Memnon's. Arrian describes this initial fighting as 'a cavalry battle with infantry tactics: horse against horse, man against man, locked together …' (Arrian I.15).

In practical application, Alexander's gaudy attire may well have been intended to make him as prominent as possible so that the Persians would come at the king first, thereby giving Parmenion and the main thrust of the Macedonian forces time to cross the river unmolested. As it turns out, Parmenion's troops were hardly needed at all. When Alexander caught sight of the charging Mithridates, he asked for a new spear – apparently, he had fought for some time with the broken one. With a new weapon provided him by Demaratus

Right: At the Granicus. Cleitus 'the Black' (centre) is shown saving Alexander (right) from the scimitar blow of the Persian satrap of Lydia, Spithridates.

of Corinth, Alexander disengaged, rallied his men, and rode straight for Mithradates and his oncoming cavalry charge. Galloping at the front of his men, Alexander struck Mithridates hard in the face with his spear, knocking him from his horse, at which point another Persian commander, Rhoesaces, fell upon Alexander, his scimitar upraised, and struck at Alexander's head. Dulled by Alexander's helmet, the crash of the Persian's scimitar, nevertheless, sliced off a portion of Alexander's head gear, leaving him dazed and vulnerable. Somehow, Alexander recovered quickly enough to fell Rhoesaces with a spear thrust to the chest. But the blow to the head stunned the Macedonian king, as he does not seem to have registered the hooves of the Persian war horse thundering up behind him. Spithridates, the satrap of Lydia and Ionia, approaching fast from Alexander's rear, raised his scimitar to deal Alexander what likely would have been his death blow, had not Cleitus 'the Black', a commander in the royal squadron of the Companions, rode in and, with one magnificent blow, sliced off Spithridates' arm at the shoulder.

At this point, a woozy Alexander may have fallen from his horse, to be surrounded swiftly and revived by members of the Companions. He was soon well enough to join the fighting again and to lead a rout of the Persian cavalry before the Macedonian heavy infantry even had a chance to join battle in earnest. With the Persian cavalry in retreat, the weaker infantry forces at the Persian centre began to crumble. The seasoned Memnon ordered the men under his command, mostly Greek mercenaries, to

Right: These line drawings show a Persian archer and spearman, after wall reliefs from Susa and Persepolis.

retreat in orderly fashion to the high ground above the plain and wait matters out. They watched as their Persian masters fled in terror before the Macedonian king.

The Fate of the Greek Mercenaries

Memnon now sent a message to Alexander asking for terms of surrender for him and his men. Alexander refused to provide any. Instead he called upon his phalanx, fully emerged from the river and still fresh from lack of serious fighting, to attack Memnon's position. Despite his heavy involvement in the earlier fighting, his extremely close call and, quite possibly, a mild concussion, Alexander led the frontal assault himself. Memnon's mercenaries fought valiantly. Alexander's refusal to offer them quarter surely meant that the king intended to show them no mercy, so they had considerable motivation to do so.

During the fighting, Alexander's horse was killed underneath him by a mercenary's spear and the king was forced to fight on foot. The fallen horse was not Bucephalus. We cannot say for sure whether Alexander switched horses

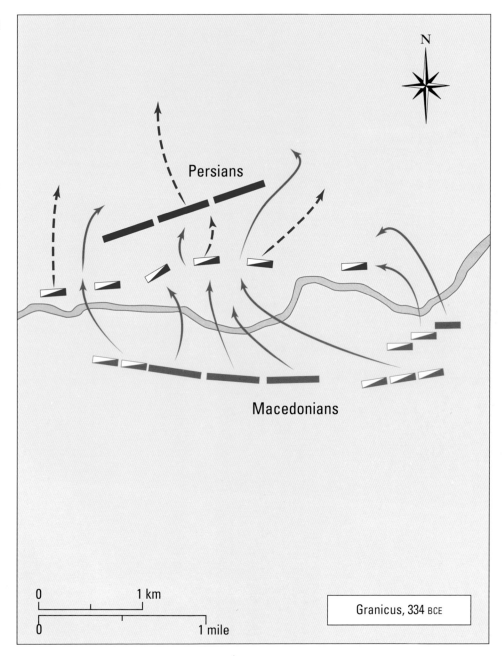

Persians

Macedonians

0   1 km

0   1 mile

Granicus, 334 BCE

before advancing against Memnon's position –
perhaps out of a healthy respect for the prowess of
the Greek mercenary general and the fear of losing
his prized stallion – or whether he did not wish
to risk Bucephalus at all in the river crossing and
ensuing close-quartered combat and, as such, rode a
different horse from the outset. If this was the case,
the Granicus is the one major battle of Alexander's
in which the Macedonian king did not ride his great
black war horse. Although his men were ultimately
defeated by the Macedonians, the slippery Memnon
managed, by some conceit, to escape and trouble
Alexander another day. Arrian tells us that a few
mercenaries may have escaped Alexander's notice
by hiding among the heaps of dead bodies (Arrian
I.16). The unheroic and humiliating ruse would
seem beneath the mighty Memnon, but it may have
saved his life, or at least preserved his freedom, for
Alexander chose to make an example of the Greek
mercenaries who fought alongside him. He may
have executed as many as 15,000 mercenaries in the
service of the Great King that day and sent another
2000 or so in chains to Macedon to work in forced
labour camps. Those men he enslaved may have
been Memnon's bravest and boldest, the fighters
who dared to make a last stand against Alexander.
The Macedonian king, as such, acknowledged their
bravery by sparing their lives. His message still rang
abundantly clear. Any Greek who chose to serve the
Great King of Persia over the rightful hegemon of
Greece would be dealt with in the harshest terms.

Arrian tells us that the Macedonian losses at the
Granicus were small. He estimates little more than

Facing page: Ruins of the Temple of Artemis at Sardis. Construction of the temple began in 334 BCE, not long after Alexander liberated the city from Persian rule. Completed about 300 BCE, Artemis' Temple at Sardis was the fourth largest Ionic temple in the world.

a hundred Macedonian dead, but these numbers are certainly low given the early fierce fighting on the river bank, and the even more intense engagement with Memnon's mercenaries later on. Whatever the number may actually have been, Alexander ordered that all of the fallen be buried in high ceremony with their arms and equipment the day after the battle and that, henceforth, their families be exempt from taxation. As for the wounded, the king showed great concern, visiting each individually, and asking every man how he received his wound. Finally, as an offering to Athena, he sent to Athens 300 full suits of Persian armour (*panoplies*) to be displayed in the temple of the goddess on the Acropolis.

Along with the Persian panoplies, he sent the following inscription, 'Alexander, son of Philip, and the Greeks (except the Lacedaemonians) dedicate these spoils taken from the Persians who dwell in Asia'. (Arrian I.17) It is interesting that Alexander included the Greeks in the inscription, who played a quite minor role in the battle, but omitted his own Macedonians. Perhaps this represents Alexander's attempt to emphasize the Greek-ness of the Macedonians or his belief that the Macedonians in fact were Greeks. Or the inscription was mere clever propaganda, intended to assure the Greek city-states that Alexander fought on their behalves and in their interests and to dissuade them from potential rebellion.

Alexander's Intentions

Having appointed the Macedonian, Calas, to the satrapy of Hellespontine Phrygia, formerly held by Arsites, Alexander sent Permenion ahead to occupy the satrapal capital at Dascylium, but otherwise left the pacification of the region in Calas' hands. Thereafter, Alexander turned his attentions south and to a significant prize, Sardis, the capital of Persian Lydia. He was still 13km (eight miles) away when the Persian commander of the citadel, Mithrines, met him on the road and surrendered the city to Alexander. Even still, little more than 3km (two miles) from Sardis, Alexander sent ahead an advance force under Amyntas, son of Andromenes, to take the fortress, suggestive of the fact that, despite being its commander, Mithrines was not convinced that the city's Persian garrison would surrender without a fight. In point of fact, they did.

For his trouble, Alexander allowed Mithrines to maintain a position 'suitable to his rank' although he appointed Pausanias, a member of the Companions, as garrison commander and placed the city proper and the satrapy of Lydia in the hands of Parmenion's brother, Asandrus. With the city of Sardis in hand, Alexander ascended the citadel, where he decided to build a temple to Zeus. As he ruminated on the precise spot where the shrine should stand, an early summer squall rolled across the city; its violent thunder and lightning Alexander took as Zeus' approval of his decision and he gave orders to erect the temple to the master of Olympus with speed.

Sardis lay at the start of the Persian Royal Road to Susa, the Achaemenids' administrative capital, a fact that certainly would not have been lost on Alexander. And here, it is worth considering for a moment whether Alexander had long-term plans for his invasion, and, if so, what they might have been. In his initial takeover of Persian territories, he did not alter the structures of government, and the Macedonians he placed in charge retained a distinctively Persian title, satrap. He specifically instructed them that taxes and tribute should not be increased, but maintained at the same level as under their Achaemenid predecessors. He offered a general amnesty to the inhabitants of Phrygia and Lydia, even those who had fought in the Persian ranks, and he even allowed some Persians, like Mithrines at Sardis, to maintain offices of some importance.

Did he truly intend to take the fight to the Persian heartland? To overthrow an empire that stretched from the Hellespont to the far side of the Hindu Kush? And to replace Darius, the Great King? Or, at this point, was his primary motivation merely to free the Greek colonies on the Aegean coast and those areas of Asia Minor in the Greek sphere of influence from the yoke of Persian rule and repay the Achaemenids the dishonour they had wrought upon the Greeks when they burned Greek temples and plundered Greek cities over a century and a half earlier during the Graeco–Persian Wars? His next move was to march southwest to Ephesus,

another important commercial and administrative centre some 113km (70 miles) from Sardis.

Alexander's troops made the journey in roughly three days. When the city's mercenary garrison learned of the Macedonian approach, they fled. No doubt word of Alexander's harsh treatment of Memnon's forces at the Granicus had circulated in the region, and, when Alexander arrived, he found the inhabitants of the city trying to round up and put to death those mercenaries who had been loyal to Memnon, a pursuit to which the Macedonian king swiftly called a halt. No sooner had Parmenion arrived from Dascylium and met up with Alexander was he dispatched again with about 5000 infantry and a single squadron of the Companion cavalry to liberate any Greek towns along the coast still subject to Persian rule.

Alexander remained in Ephesus briefly and offered sacrifice at the city's ancient temple of

Left: Facade of the Library of Celsus at Ephesus, named and built for Tiberius Julius Celsus Polemaeanus (c. 45–119 CE), Roman consul in 92 CE, governor of Asian provinces thereafter, and prominent citizen and *euergetes* ('benefactor') of the city. The library was built by Celsus' son as a kind of monument and mausoleum. It was comprised of three stories and held more than 12,000 volumes. Celsus' remains lay in a sarcophagus beneath the building.

Facing page: The celebrated Greek artist, Apelles, painting Campaspe (a mistress of Alexander and Larissan aristocrat) as Alexander looks on, by Pietro Bagatti Valsecchi (1832), oil on canvas.

Above: The torsion catapult. Used to great effect by Philip II and Alexander, the powerful, torque-propelled catapult helped the Macedonians to revolutionize siege warfare.

Artemis, after which he held a grand parade of his troops, fully arrayed in battle order. The Ephesian populace cheered him as liberator.

Before departing Ephesus, Alexander learned that the celebrated painter, Apelles, was in residence there. Alexander had a portrait commissioned of himself atop Bucephalus. Although Alexander had heard of Apelles' fame, he was very much disappointed with the finished product. Apelles thereafter asked that Bucephalus

be brought to the studio and placed beside the picture, and the great war horse nickered at his resemblance, at which Apelles suggested that perhaps the horse was a better judge of art than the king. Apelles' apprentices giggled, but Alexander held his temper and merely insisted that the artist try again. The result was a highly propagandist rendering of the Macedonian king wielding a thunderbolt, Zeus-like.

The Siege of Miletus

Leaving Ephesus, Alexander's next stop was Miletus. He faced resistance there, a city where large numbers of mercenaries had been stationed. The Persian garrison commander appeared to be waiting on the arrival of the Persian fleet and reinforcements. The Persian fleet did, in fact, arrive and anchored some distance from the city near Mount Mycale. But Alexander's fleet, commanded by Nearchus, had already seized the position beside the island of Lade, directly in front of Miletus' harbour. Although the Persians had 400 ships, more than twice the Macedonian number, the Persians' inability to anchor in the main harbour effectively made them spectators from the foothills of Mount Mycale, 15km (nine miles) away. Alexander, therefore, had ample time to employ his siege artillery.

Macedonian siegecraft had been improved greatly under Philip, whose innovation of the torsion catapult (*katapeltai*), which allowed missiles to fly faster and farther than ever before in the Greek world, could be employed to devastating

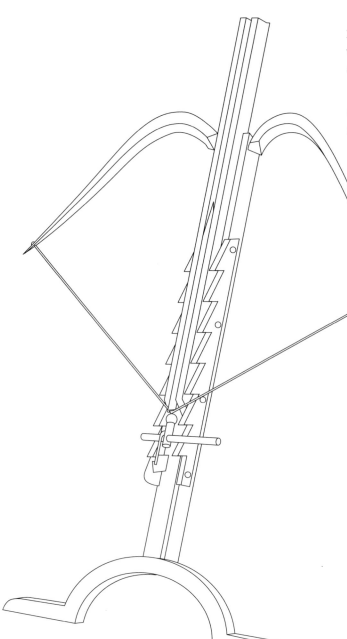

Left: The *gastraphetes* or 'belly-shooter', so-called because it was cocked on the ground against the stomach and braced against the abdomen when fired.

effect against a walled city. Diodorus' description of Philip's siege of Perinthus, in 340 BCE, provides valuable information, not only about the artillery at Philip's disposal, but the manner in which a siege would have been carried out by the Macedonians. Philip also employed battering rams with metal heads that shook the walls of gates and cities and teams of miners to dig trenches beneath them. In addition to the powerful torsion catapult, the Macedonians probably fired upon cities by means of the *gastraphetes* (belly-shooter), a kind of proto-crossbow, cocked by the use of the stomach. The process created more tension and ultimately velocity in the flight of the missile than with a traditional bow. Manipulated by strong-men specialists, the *gastraphetes* shot a large, three-pronged arrow at a considerable distance.

Macedonian siege towers stood 35.5m (120ft) high, and what is more impressive is that they arrived at the site in prefabricated pieces to be assembled by a corps of professional engineers. Because Philip's siege towers often stood far taller than the towers of besieged cities, the besieging army enjoyed a tactical advantage and the ability to wear down the besieged by a constant rain of arrows and missiles from on high. More than any specific siege technology, Philip's most important contribution to Macedonian siege warfare was the institution of the permanent, highly-trained corps of engineers, who assembled, positioned and manned the siege machinery on site. The Macedonian corps of engineers and Philip's commitment to perfecting the art of siege warfare made him unique and feared in the Greek world, and created for Alexander the means by which he might bring even great cities to heel.

After a brief siege, Alexander successfully took the city of Miletus, and pardoned the Milesians themselves, who claimed to have been forced into resistance by the Persian garrison. Alexander thereafter made the city a member of the League of Corinth with full rights and privileges. Although their presence had been a great help to Alexander at Miletus, the king disbanded the greater portion of his fleet, maintaining a mere twenty ships. Alexander's action has puzzled historians, although most believe that the disbanding of the Macedonian fleet represents a tacit admission by the king that the Persians were superior at sea and that he did not wish to risk pitched battle with the Persian navy. Arrian adds that the king had not the money to maintain the fleet and that he understood that, once the towns upon the Asian coast had fallen into Macedonian hands, the Persian presence at sea would be rendered impotent (Arrian I.20).

The Return of Memnon

From Miletus, Alexander travelled along the coast to Halicarnassus, capital of the Persian satrapy

The Macedonian Siege of Perinthus

'Philip, whose fortunes were constantly on the increase, made an expedition against Perinthus, which had resisted him and inclined toward the Athenians. He instituted a siege and advancing engines to the city assailed the walls in relays day after day. He built towers eighty cubits (35.5m/120ft) high, which far overtopped the towers of Perinthus, and from a superior height kept wearing down the besieged. He rocked the walls with battering rams and undermined them with saps, and cast down a long stretch of wall. The Perinthians fought stoutly in their own defence and quickly threw up a second wall; many admirable feats were performed in the open and on the fortifications. Both sides displayed great determination. The king, for his part, rained destruction with numerous and varied catapults upon the men fighting steadfastly along the battlements, while the Perinthians, although their daily losses were heavy, received reinforcements of men, missiles and artillery from Byzantium. When they had again become a match for the enemy, they took courage and resolutely bore the brunt of the battle for their homeland. Still the king persevered in his determination. He divided his forces into several divisions and with reliefs kept up a continuous attack on the walls both day and night. He had 30,000 men and a store of missiles and siege engines besides machines in plenty, and kept up a steady pressure against the besieged people' (Diodorus Siculus XVI.74).

Above: Artist's rendering of a Macedonian siege tower, which would have been built of prefabricated pieces at the site of a siege to stand about 35.5m (120ft) high.

Facing page: The Myndos Gate at ancient Halicarnassus (modern Bodrum), site of Alexander's siege of the city in 334 BCE.

of Caria, where he would face stiff resistance, for Memnon of Rhodes, having been given supreme command of the Asian coast and the Persian fleet, had arrived personally to undertake the defence of the city. Alexander expected the city to be betrayed into his hands and was perhaps not counting on the presence of Memnon. His corps of engineers and siege artillery had tarried at Miletus and, when he arrived outside the walls at Halicarnassus, Alexander was not prepared for a protracted siege. He had his infantry begin digging trenches to undermine the city walls, but they faced considerable resistance and were forced to withdraw.

When the Macedonian siege machinery did arrive, the Halicarnassians launched a night-time surprise attack, in an attempt to set fire to the Macedonian siege engines. An intense battle ensued that left some 16 Macedonians killed, and more than 300 wounded, but Alexander's artillery was intact. Memnon's night attack was a cunning ploy, but its failure meant Alexander would indeed move his siege engines into position and begin pelting the city with the full complement of his arsenal. At this point, Memnon recognized that it was only a matter of time before the city fell to the Macedonian onslaught. He evacuated his men from the city, again slipping through Alexander's fingers, to the island of Cos.

MAVSOLÆVM.

The Mausoleum of Halicarnassus

In addition to her husband and brother, Idrieus, Ada of Caria was sister to Mausolus and Artemesia II, the famed sibling lovers and dynasts of Caria. Artemesia, upon Mausolus' death, had erected the great Mausoleum of Halicarnassus, named for her husband. Determined to build for her deceased lover a monument that would bring everlasting fame to his name and family, she employed the finest Greek artists and artisans, pouring enormous resources into the construction of a building that would gain such renown that it would become one of the Seven Wonders of the Ancient World and give its name to all monumental tombs thereafter. During his siege of Halicarnassus, which did significant damage to the city, Alexander left the great Mausoleum untouched. This is reminiscent of Alexander's treatment of the home of Pindar during the razing of Thebes. The Mausoleum would stand intact until at least the twelfth century CE, more than 1500 years after its construction.

No doubt concerned about the return of Memnon, Alexander garrisoned the city with 3000 infantry and about 200 mounted troops under the command of Ptolemy. To the governorship of the province of Caria, he appointed Ada, an aging princess of the Carian dynastic line, the Hecatomnids, who, in the wake of her husband and brother's death, had formerly ruled as a kind of tributary regent for the Persians, before being exiled to the fortress of Alinda on the outskirts of Caria. Ada had met Alexander on the road as he entered her province, paid him due homage, and surrendered her city of Alinda to the king. She even offered to adopt Alexander, a proposal that he readily accepted, not only as a gesture of respect to Ada, but to ensure that, upon her death, rightful control of the region would pass to him and not some would-be tyrant or satrap with potential ties to the Great King of Persia. Clearly, Alexander had serious concerns about the continuing security of the region, because only by maintaining control of the coastal cities of Miletus and Halicarnassus could he neutralize the Persian navy and the ongoing threat of Memnon.

For his part, Memnon had captured the islands of Chios and Lesbos, and was distributing money to the cities of mainland Greece in the hopes of fostering dissention there. He now intended to sail to Greece with 300 ships and to strike at the heart of Alexander's power, the second phase of the plan he had proposed at the war council at Zeleia. When news of Memnon's intentions reached mainland Greece, some in the city-states, and especially the Spartans, seemed ready to welcome Memnon's arrival, but at the very moment when the great mercenary general seemed poised to deal Alexander the first significant setback of his career, Memnon fell ill and died, and his plans to invade Greece were shelved.

Facing page: The Tomb of Mausolus or 'Mausoleum' at Halicarnassus, one of the Seven Wonders of the Ancient World, after a painting by Maarten van Heemskerck, 1572.

Below: Artemisia II, dynast of Caria, inspects plans for the Mausoleum of Halicarnassus. Painting by Simon Vouet (1590–1649), oil on canvas.

Below: The Taurus Mountains, which separate southern Anatolia's (modern Turkey's) Mediterranean coastal region from the central Anatolian Plateau. Alexander marched through the Taurus range to reach the city of Tarsus.

Alexander's Illness

With winter upon him, Alexander stopped and rested at Gordium before turning his gaze, in spring, to another important coastal city, one of the main ports of southern Asia Minor, the city of Tarsus. But getting to Tarsus with his massive force would be no small task, for the city was surrounded by the craggy peaks of Mt. Taurus some 914m (3000ft high). Alexander reached the Taurus range in summer 333 BCE, and ordered forced marches through the mountains. As the king emerged into open country, sweating and exhausted, he stripped naked and plunged into the cold waters of the river Cydnus. Thereafter, he developed a cramp that became increasingly debilitating. Although he took Tarsus without incident, Arrian tells us that Alexander's ill-advised swim in the Cydnus had led to a severe illness that included violent convulsions and raging fever. His physicians and intimates feared the worst.

One can imagine that Alexander's sickness could have been caused by any number of factors beyond a mere dip in a cold river. The whirlwind campaigns and long marches of more than a year had surely taken their toll on the young king and his body may have collapsed from sheer exhaustion. Only one doctor, Philip of Acarnania, a long-time friend of Alexander, held out hope for his recovery from his mysterious illness and stood by his side, administering various pharmacological and holistic treatments to the king even as Parmenion claimed to have received intelligence that, in fact, Philip was trying to poison Alexander, an accusation that Alexander nonchalantly dismissed. Whatever the case may be, and whatever Alexander's illness might have been, Philip's treatments and Alexander's robust constitution pulled him through. But he had been bedridden for nearly three months at Tarsus, a convalescence that allowed Darius, the Great King,

to regroup and to formulate a new strategy to defeat his Macedonian opponent, a strategy that now included the Great King leading his army in person.

Alexander certainly realized as much. For this reason, Parmenion had been occupied during much of the period of Alexander's infirmity. The Macedonian king had been savvy enough to send the old general ahead to scout Darius' movements, to block the passes and, in general, to secure the region for the Macedonians. He commanded a force made up almost entirely of Greek mercenaries and Thracian and Thessalian horsemen. Alexander must have wished to retain the greater part of the Macedonian army at Tarsus to protect the coast from the Persian navy, although Alexander's troops, no doubt, stood ready to advance to Parmenion's position should word arrive that Darius was on the move.

With Alexander finally on the mend, he received the communication for which he had been waiting. After capturing the small harbour town of Issus, Parmenion had obtained confirmation that Darius was encamped with a large army two days march from the Pillar of Jonah, near the Syrian Gates. Toward that end, he set up a Macedonian base of operations at Issus.

Planning the Campaign of Issus

At last well enough to leave Tarsus, Alexander proceeded southwest to the town of Soli, where he faced guerrilla-style skirmishes in the surrounding foothills. Having barely recovered from his illness, Alexander was in no mood to be trifled with, and

Left: Darius III, the last Great King of Achaemenid Persia (r. 336–330 BCE). A detail from the Alexander Mosaic from House of the Faun, Pompeii.

Left: Alexander addresses his men before the Battle of Issus, where he would meet Darius III on the field for the first time (from a nineteenth-century illustration).

having dealt with the skirmishers, he returned to Soli and imposed a fine of 200 silver talents for the town's resistance and on-going support of Persia. There, he received good news from Halicarnassus, which had been briefly retaken by the Persian commander, Orontobates. Ptolemy's forces had managed to defeat Orontobates in pitched battle and to firmly secure the region for the Macedonians. In thanksgiving for this success and his miraculous recovery, Alexander made sacrifice at Soli to Asclepius, the god of medicine and healing. Next he crossed the Aleian plain, first to Megarsus and then to Mallus on the Pyramus River, which he found in a state of anarchy and rebellion against the Great King. Alexander quickly settled the political upheavals and remitted the tribute that the Mallians had been complaining about back to the people of the colony, on the grounds that Mallus was originally a colony of Argos and that he himself was descended from the Argive, Heracles. At Mallus, Alexander received word that the Persian army was on the move again, and he immediately called his marshals, including Parmenion, Philotas and Ptolemy, to a war council to construct a plan for confronting Darius.

At this point our sources diverge, but it seems clear that there was some delay before the two armies met in battle, perhaps a period of two weeks or so. Each army may have been waiting

the other out, assuming a defensive posture. Darius, in particular, whose army was encamped at Sochoi, desired to meet Alexander on the plains to take advantage of his superior numbers. He may have had as many as 90,000 or 100,000 troops at his disposal, a force that would have numbered more than twice Alexander's men. At Alexander's war council, it was decided that the Macedonian army would move south along the Syrian coast as far as the Belen Pass at Myriandrus, passing through Issus and Parmenion's base to drop off their wounded as they did so. Alexander hoped to lure Darius into the narrows of the Belen Pass or the Pillar of Jonah, where the Macedonians could either cut the Persians off or, if they successfully emerged from the pass, fight on a narrow coastal strip between the Amanus Mountains and the sea. In either case, Alexander would have denied Darius his numerical advantage.

Darius instead ordered his army to move north around the Amanus range, ultimately entering the city of Issus without opposition. Darius proceeded, unceremoniously, to cut off the hands of the Macedonian wounded as well as Alexander's supply lines. In the glee of this achievement, however, Darius had not realized, at least until his scouts informed him, that Alexander's army was in view. The Great King would still be forced to fight on

Left: The Deli Cay River (possibly the ancient Pinarus), near the modern Turkish–Syrian border, thought by some scholars to be the site of the Battle of Issus. Others, however, have argued that the Pinarus is the nearby Payas River.

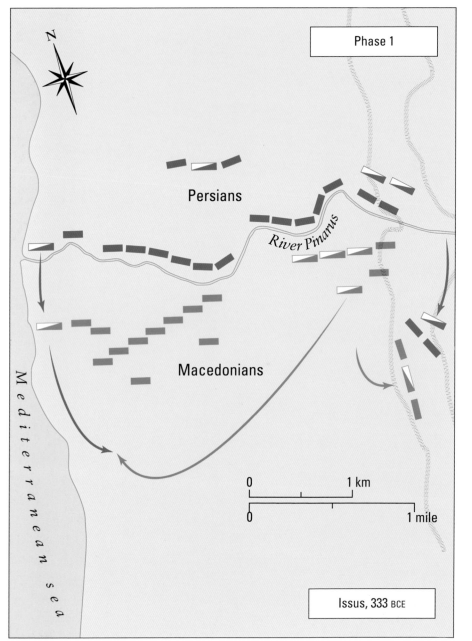

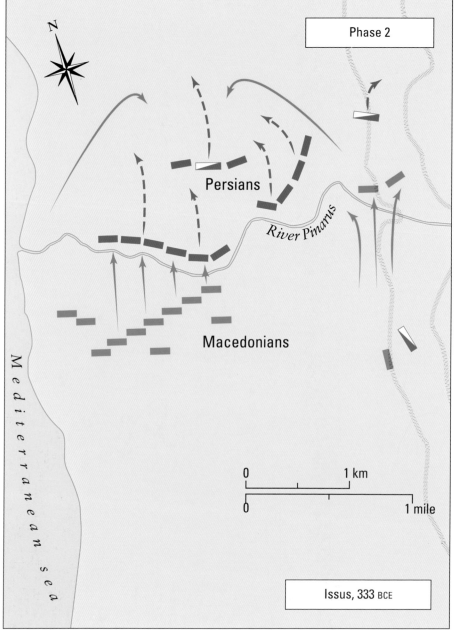

Alexander's terms, on a narrow strip of coast flanked by the Amanus Mountains and the Pinarus River near the Gulf of Issus.

With Darius encamped near the Pinarus, Alexander gathered his troops and gave a rousing speech. He talked of the many dangers that they had endured and overcome together, about the fact that *they* were free men, and that the Persian army, with its multitude of mercenaries, were mere slaves to a gluttonous, spendthrift king, that they fought for Greece – and with their hearts – whereas the Persians fought for pay or out of fear. Beyond that, he concluded, 'and what, finally, of the two men in supreme command? You have Alexander, they – Darius' (Arrian II.7). After the speech, Alexander ordered his men to eat, after which he prayed and made sacrifice to the sea nymph, Thetis, mother of his ancestor, Achilles. When night fell, Alexander sent an advance force to secure the heights and the rocky ground above the narrow pass near the Pillar of Jonah.

King versus King

By dawn, the high ground was in Macedonian hands and the main force of Alexander's army marched 16km (10 miles) north toward Darius'

Facing page: This diagram shows two phases of the Battle of Issus. The Persian line consisted of cavalry on the right, with hoplites and *kardakes* (Persian heavy infantry) in the centre and a further force of infantry to the right. Alexander's archers were able to repel the Persian attack while his cavalry crossed the river with a successful outflanking manoeuvre.

Left: 'The Battle of Alexander at Issus' by German artist, Albrecht Altdorfer (1480–1538). Alte Pinakothek, Munich.

Above: The Battle of Issus. Darius is pictured at left fleeing in his war chariot (illustration by Dudley Tennant, from *The Outline of History,* Volume 1, by H.G. Wells, published 1920).

retreat back across the river and attempt to act as reinforcements for the arrayed army of the Great King. When the battle was joined, Alexander led the Companion cavalry over the Pinarus, and, riding at the apex of his lethal wedge formation, he charged the left wing of his Persian opponents. Although the Persian lines waivered, Alexander himself received a wound in the thigh.

Parmenion, along with the heavy infantry and the Thracian and Thessalian horse on the left, had encountered even more difficulty, for, as they ascended the steep bank of the river, they lost formation and created a gap in their lines, which the Greek mercenaries on the Persian right immediately exploited. A fierce struggle ensued at the river's edge. Meanwhile, Alexander and the Companions, having broken through the enemy left, were hurling themselves at the Persian centre, at Darius and his magnificent war chariot. Here, the Great King himself likely decided the outcome of the battle.

When he saw Alexander approaching furiously, he turned his chariot and fled. Alexander's first inclination was to pursue, for it would only be with Darius' fall or capture that Achaemenid Persia would belong to Macedon. But the Macedonian left was struggling to hold its own against Persia's hardened, hired mercenaries, who seemed bent on proving to the Macedonians that even Greeks who fought in the service of the Great King were still the finest warriors in the wider Mediterranean. At any rate, Darius had quickly exchanged his chariot for a horse, cast off his royal cloak and galloped apace northward beyond Alexander's

position. According to Arrian, when word came of Alexander's approach, Darius showed signs of panic, sending an advance contingent of cavalry and light infantry across the river to hold off Alexander while he hurriedly ordered the main body of his army into battle formation. During the actual battle, this Persian advance force would

reach, at least for the moment. Alexander and the Companions now turned to give aid to the ranks of Parmenion. Almost upon their arrival in the thick of the fighting, word ran through the Persian lines that the Great King had fled. The news threw the Persian forces into disarray and the Battle of Issus was effectively over.

The moment Alexander realized the battle was won, he took Ptolemy and a small contingent and rode hard on the heels of the fleeing Darius. But, at nightfall, his prize having evaded him, Alexander broke off the pursuit and returned to the Pinarus and to heaps of enemy dead. Here, he commandeered the Great King's camp and its extravagant booty, none more valuable than the family of the Great King himself, Darius' wife, Stateira, the queen mother, Sisygambis, and his three children. Alexander treated them with the utmost dignity. He honoured Stateira and Sisygambis as he would any queen and ordered his men to do the same. His victory had been decisive, but 8000 Greek mercenaries had escaped into the hills and he had not captured or killed the Great King, who, if he could make it to the Persian heartland unencumbered, would use the enormous resources in the Persian treasury to buy himself one more chance against Alexander.

Left: 'Battle of Arbelles in 333 BCE', by the French School, a seventeenth-century Aubusson tapestry. Although the artists have titled the painting 'Battle of Arbelles', meaning Arbela (Gaugamela), they have also given the year of the Battle of Issus (333).

From Issus to Gaugamela

As dawn broke on the day following the Battle of Issus, Alexander awoke as the victor in pitched combat against the Great King. He was 3000 talents richer, the fruits of commandeering Darius' baggage train, but also in his possession, and far more valuable than material resources perhaps, were the Great King's wife, mother and children.

S o, as the sun rose, Alexander and his most intimate friends paid a visit to the royal ladies. The king and Hephaestion were said to be dressed alike, except that Hephaestion was slightly taller than Alexander, and even more handsome. Sisygambis, the mother of Darius, mistook Hephaestion for the king and fell to her knees in obeisance. While the other members in

Alexander's retinue and one of her own attendants scurried to correct the queen mother's mistake, Alexander interjected, 'Never mind Mother. For, actually, he too is Alexander' (Diodorus Siculus XXXVII.6). Alexander would, thereafter, ratify formally his adoption by Sisygambis. His statement regarding Hephaestion is perhaps even more interesting, and points either to the nature of his intimate and long-standing relationship with his childhood friend, to Alexander's acknowledgement that all of his commanders were, to some degree or another, as important as he, or perhaps, to the fact that Alexander was satisfied by the mere admission by Sisygambis that *Alexander*

Facing page: The Battle of Gaugamela, 331 BCE: Alexander the Great defeats the Persians under Darius III (by seventeenth-century artist Charles le Brun).

Right: Alexander the Great with the shield and armour of Achilles (bottom left), Roman engraved glass, first century BCE.

Above: 'The Clemency of Alexander the Great in front of the Family of Darius III', by Venetian painter Giovanni Antonio Pelligrini (1675–1741), oil on canvas.

happily return to Darius his wife, mother and children, if only the Great King would come to him, pay him due homage and acknowledge him as lord of Asia. He also suggested that, in future, Darius should refrain from writing to him 'as to an equal'. For, in Alexander's words, 'everything you possess is now mine …' (Arrian II.15).

Alexander marched into Phoenicia and the cities of Byblos and Sidon opened their gates to him. The Phoenicians were a proud people, possessed of a dynamic legacy. They had been the ancient world's first great mariners, and had devised the Mediterranean's first true alphabet, but Sidon, in particular, had suffered under Persian rule, perhaps due in no small part to the Great King's marked patronage of her sister city at Tyre, which continued to be a flourishing commercial and cultural centre under the Achaemenids. In fact, Tyre had grown to the extent that she had become two cities, Old Tyre, on the Phoenician mainland, and New Tyre, a shining island metropolis that had grown up around the formidable sanctuary of the Tyrian god, Melqart.

The new island city was largely the result of the financial boom the Tyrians had enjoyed under Persian rule, as they maintained a kind of trade monopoly along the Syrian coast. When Alexander asked to make a sacrifice to the indigenous Tyrian deity, Melqart, who was associated with his ancestor Heracles, the Tyrians, recognizing that allowing the Macedonian king entrance to Melqart's shrine in the new city would effectively amount to acclaiming him, and not Darius, their king, refused. The Tyrians wish to hedge their bets and remain neutral

was now her king regardless of who that Alexander precisely was.

After Alexander's victory at Issus, he looked to secure firmly the Syrian coast, beginning with a march south to Marathus and into Phoenicia. He sent Parmenion east to Damascus, a move that suggests his intent to carry the fight to the Persian heartland. At Marathus, he received a letter from Darius requesting the release of his family. Alexander wrote back, responding that he would

in the on-going fight between Macedon and Persia led Alexander to undertake the most protracted siege of his career.

The Siege of Tyre

While Alexander took the old city with relative ease, New Tyre, on an island 800m (half a mile) from shore, surrounded by waters 183m (600ft) deep and walls 46m (150ft) tall, an unusual height by ancient standards, would be another matter altogether. To lay siege effectively to the island city, Alexander would be forced to build a causeway that connected the mainland to the island and erect two 52m (170ft) tall siege towers, the tallest recorded in Mediterranean and Near Eastern history to date. Out of spite or necessity, Alexander demolished much of the old city, and used the rubble as building materials for the siege mole.

The further the causeway extended into deep water, the more vulnerable Alexander's engineers became to attacks from the Phoenician fleet. Alexander's naval power was limited, so he sent for assistance from nearby Rhodes and Cyprus. The Rhodians would arrive quickly, but their ten triremes made a minimal difference in the proceedings. The Tyrians had powerful naval allies, as well, in their North African colony at Carthage, a city and people not far from becoming a formidable

Left: 'Sisygambis, mother of Darius III, mistakes Hephistion (Hephaestion) for Alexander the Great' by late-Baroque, Neoclassicist painter, Francesco de Mura (1696–1782).

Letters between Alexander and Darius

Darius to Alexander: 'Philip and Artaxerxes (III 'Ochus') were on terms of friendship and alliance; but upon the accession of Artaxeres' son Arses, Philip was guilty of unprovoked aggression against him. Now, since Darius' reign began, Alexander has sent no representative to his court to confirm the former friendship and alliance between the two kingdoms; on the contrary, he has crossed into Asia with his armed forces and done much damage to the Persians. For this reason Darius took the field in defence of his country and ancestral throne. The issue of the battle was as some god willed; and now Darius the king asks Alexander the king to restore from captivity his wife, his mother, and his children, and is willing to make friends with him and be his ally. For this cause he urges Alexander to send to him, in company with Meniscus and Arsimas who have brought this request, representatives of his own in order that proper guarantees may be exchanged'.

Alexander to Darius: 'Your ancestors invaded Macedonia and Greece and caused havoc in our country, though we had done nothing to provoke them. As supreme commander of all Greece I invaded Asia because I wished to punish Persia for this act – an act which must be laid wholly to your charge. You sent aid to the people of Perinthus in their rebellion against my father; Ochus sent an army into Thrace, which was part of our dominions; my father was killed by assassins whom, as you openly

Above: Alexander the Great receives messengers from Darius III, illustration from thirteenth-century (Nerses) manuscript of 'The Romance of Alexander.'

boasted in your letters, you yourselves hired to commit the crime; having murdered Arses with Bagoas' help, you unjustly and illegally seized the throne, thereby committing a crime against your country; you sent the Greeks false information about me in the hope of making them my enemy; you attempted to supply the Greeks with money – which only the Lacedaemonians were willing to accept, your agents corrupted my friends and tried to wreck the peace which I had established in Greece – then it was that I took the field against you; but it was you who began the quarrel. First I defeated in battle your generals and satraps; now I have defeated yourself and the army you led. By the Gods help I am master of your country, and I have made myself responsible for the survivors of your army who fled to me for refuge: far from being detained by force, they are serving of their own free will under my command.

'Come to me, therefore, as you would come to the lord of the continent of Asia. Should you fear to suffer any indignity at my hands, then send some of your friends and I will give them proper guarantees. Come, then, and ask me for your mother, your wife and your children and anything else you please; for you shall have them, and whatever besides you can persuade me to give you.

'And in future let any communication you wish to make with me be addressed to the King of all Asia. Do not write to me as an equal. Everything you possess is now mine; so, if you should want anything, let me know in proper terms, or I shall take steps to deal with you as a criminal. If, on the other hand, you wish to dispute your throne, stand and fight for it and do not run away. Wherever you may hide yourself, be sure I shall seek you out.' (Cf. Arrian 2.14)

Mediterranean power in their own right. As both Tyre and Alexander awaited further assistance at sea, the Tyrians managed to destroy Alexander's great siege towers almost as soon as they were constructed, by sending horse galleys (large ships used to transport cavalry horses) packed with

straw, kindling, and pitch and setting them afire by long-range arrows to burst into flames upon colliding with the Macedonian siege engines. In addition, they sent smaller vessels loaded with archers and slingers to constantly rain missiles on Alexander's engineers.

Above: Alexander's mole with its great siege towers advances towards Tyre, while the defenders shoot flaming arrows in an attempt to halt its progress.

As a result, the Macedonians suffered heavy losses, at least until the king arrived at the idea to jury-rig a protective screen of tautly-pulled tanned hides and canvas on either side of the mole to block oncoming missiles as his engineers rebuilt the siege towers, which were then manned to return fire upon the Tyrian galleys. It was a rigorous game of cat-and-mouse, with each side working furiously to outmanoeuvre the other. About this time, both Diodorus and Curtius report that a giant sea monster slammed into the causeway, an incident that both sides interpreted as a favourable omen. For their part, the Tyrians held celebratory feasts and fire dances throughout the night, convinced, as they were, that Alexander's siege project would soon fall to ruin (Curtius IV.4, Diodorus Siculus XVII.41).

Unfortunately, when the hung-over Tyrians awoke the next morning and manned their galleys, still garlanded from the previous night's revels, 120 Cypriot warships appeared on the horizon. Their coming would put an effective end to the Tyrians' ability to thwart the rapid construction of the mole. But Alexander would have one more obstacle still to overcome in the form of a gale-force wind that blew in from the northwest, pelting the causeway and the battlements that Alexander had erected, and hurling some of them into the deep surrounding waters.

Facing page: The ruins of ancient Byblos, on the coast of modern Lebanon. Byblos is thought to be the oldest city in Phoenicia and, perhaps, the oldest continuously-inhabited city in the world.

Left: Alexander commands his army at the siege of Tyre, 332 BCE (artwork from a nineteenth-century magazine).

Right: **Macedonian soldiers storm the defences at Tyre in a painting by Tom Lovell.**

With the Tyrians at bay, had Poseidon himself now conspired to deny Alexander his prize?

The City is Stormed

Alexander would not be deterred. He ordered full-grown cedar trees to be felled and floated into position to block the on-coming winds. Within weeks, with the mole completed and his siege craft in place, Alexander began his assault on the island fortress in earnest. Before the Tyrians' Carthaginian allies could set sail, Alexander had breached the walls of the city by means of a torsion catapult. At any rate, at least one member of the Carthaginian assembly, perhaps seeing the writing on the wall, begged his Carthaginian brethren not to intervene, claiming that in a dream he had seen a god leaving Tyre, perhaps Ba'al or Melqart, although Greek sources generally say Apollo, an omen that even Phoenician deities had resigned themselves to Alexander's ascendance.

When Alexander at last entered the city, he at once made a sacrifice to Melqart, as he originally intended, and dedicated to him the very catapult that had first penetrated the island stronghold. He left an inscription in the temple as well, which must have been obscene because Ptolemy and, by extension, Arrian, refused to repeat it. When he reached the temple, he found hiding there Azimilik, the Tyrian king, and the heads of other noble families, along with Carthaginian ambassadors who had found themselves trapped amidst the fighting. In a gesture of honour to Melqart (or to Heracles perhaps in Alexander's mind), Alexander spared all their lives, but he sold some 30,000 of the city's remaining citizens into slavery. Next, the king

Left: Tyrian defenders would have held up screens to protect their archers from volleys of incoming missiles.

Below: A typical Greek *trireme* was equipped with 170 oars, divided into three banks (with one rower per oar) and a bronze ram (*embolon*) at the prow. The ram was used to assault and breach the hull of enemy ships. The objective was either to sink or, more likely, to cripple or immobilize an enemy vessel, after which it could be boarded and commandeered by Greek marines.

threw a grand ceremonial parade of his troops in full battle gear. He followed the parade with lavish funeral games to honour the Macedonian dead. They included various athletic contests and torch races, the whole affair culminating in a grand feast. It was midsummer 332 BCE. The ordeal that was the siege of Tyre had lasted eight months and cost Alexander many precious lives, especially among his corps of engineers. But, as at many points in Alexander's career, the Macedonian king had demonstrated a singular persistence, even in the face of overwhelming obstacles and at high cost.

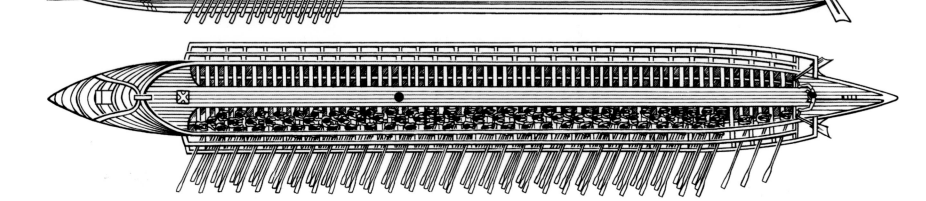

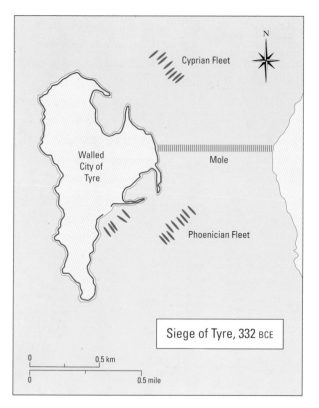

Siege of Tyre, 332 BCE

Above: Diagram of the Siege of Tyre, showing Alexander's mole (in red) with Cypriot ships (allied to Alexander) to the north and Phoenician (Tyrian) ships to the south.

Right: Roman triumphal arch and colonnaded street, Tyre Al Bass archaeological site, ancient Tyre, modern Lebanon.

Palestine and Egypt

Alexander now marched south into Palestine, 257km (160 miles) from Tyre to Gaza. The march took about 11 days. Alexander knew Gaza to be a formidable, walled stronghold at the edge of the desert, an important trade centre on an ancient caravan route. Some of its inhabitants were wealthy traders with considerable resources to defend the city even without the intervention of the Great King of Persia. Alexander had sent Hephaestion ahead by sea with the fleet that now contained his original core of ships plus the Rhodians and Cypriots that

Modern Tyre: A City Built on Alexander's Foundations

The core of the causeway that Alexander built of rubble and stone to connect the mainland to the island city of New Tyre, endures, to this day, beneath the streets of modern Tyre, the fourth largest city in the Republic of Lebanon. The modern city comprises much of the island that Alexander fought so desperately to claim. The remainder of the island is scattered with the ruins and vestiges of the once great, ancient city's splendour.

had come to his aid at Tyre. Legend has it that on the way, Alexander made a point to visit Jerusalem and to make sacrifice to Yahweh, although some scholars write off this visit as apocryphal. The siege of Gaza lasted two months and presented Alexander with new logistical difficulties as the city was effectively surrounded by desert and water was difficult to acquire.

The small wells outside Gaza's walls would have been inadequate to supply the water necessary to sustain the Macedonian forces for two months, whereas the larger wells that would have served to do so, were 50km (31 miles) away at Beersheba. The

Right: A satellite photo of Tyre today. The island has become absorbed into the mainland since ancient times.

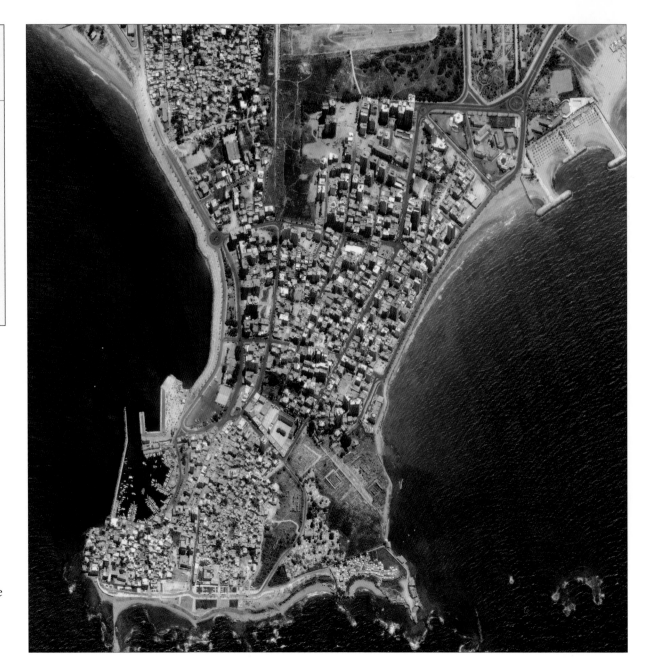

sandy soil around the city walls also complicated the positioning of siege craft, and the city was only taken by way of Alexander's impressive mining efforts. In the assault, Alexander was wounded twice, once in the shoulder by a catapult bolt and, again, in the leg in the final push to take the city. When the city did fall into Macedonian hands, Alexander's increasingly testy troops massacred the men of fighting age and took the women and children as war booty. Curtius preserves a story that Gaza's garrison commander was captured and executed in spectacularly gruesome fashion. His heels pierced, he was attached to the back of a chariot and dragged through the city streets until dead (Curtius IV.6.25–29).

Alexander now looked south to Egypt, which, according to Arrian, was 'the original object of his southerly march …' (Arrian III.1). The king moved along the coast of Sinai from Gaza to Pelusium. The dunes would have forced the army to march close to the sea or risk having the horses and baggage animals sink in the sand. The fleet would have shadowed the land army down the coast. Alexander arrived on the Egyptian border in seven days, covering a distance of about 220km (137 miles). Pelusium was a great fortress on the eastern edge of the Nile Delta, with an ample harbour to receive the Macedonian fleet. Alexander may have readied himself to face resistance from the great

Left: Siege of Gaza by the army of Alexander the Great in 332 BCE. View from Macedonian siege tower. On the lower left, a torsion catapult is readied to fire at the city wall.

fortress, Egypt's first line of defence against would-be invaders. But this would not be the case. Instead, Egyptians flocked by the thousands to Pelusium to welcome Alexander and hail him as a liberator. He gave orders to the fleet to sail up the Nile toward Memphis, setting out himself with the land army south along the river's eastern bank and stopping at Heliopolis.

There, he crossed the river and entered the ancient city of Memphis, where he immediately offered sacrifice to Apis, Egypt's sacred bull-god, associated with the indigenous Memphian deity, Ptah, and the Egyptian lord of the underworld, Osiris. Alexander's sacrifice to Apis was a nod both to the city of Memphis and her ancient patron deity, and to Egyptian religion, in general.

After making sacrifice, Alexander held games that included both athletic and literary competitions. Amid the celebrations, the Egyptians hailed Alexander as pharaoh and accorded him the traditional nomenclature of Egypt's divine king: king of Upper and Lower Egypt, beloved of Amun and chosen of Ra, son of Ra, and the human incarnation of the hawk-headed god Horus. One source (Pseudo-Callisthenes, I.34.2) even records a grand investiture ceremony and enthronement at Memphis, the practical facts of which are impossible to discern. From Memphis, Alexander sailed down river (north) to Canopus near Lake Mareotis, where he was struck by a pristine stretch of land near the sea. Here, he would found one of the ancient world's greatest cities, Egyptian Alexandria.

Above: Alexander is depicted meeting and showing deference to the Jewish high priest outside Yahweh's Temple in Jerusalem. Scholars are divided as to whether such a meeting ever actually took place.

The Siwah Oracle

At this time, Alexander also became eager to visit the oasis of Siwah in Libya, with its celebrated sanctuary to Ammon. It is somewhat difficult to disentangle the identity of the god of this shrine at Siwah, whether it be the old Theban civic god, Amun, who became an Egyptian national deity conflated with Ra after the overthrow of the Hyksos in the sixteenth century BCE, or the Syrio-

Below: Limestone grave stele, depicting the deceased (on the right) praying to the sacred Apis bull (centre), associated with Memphian Ptah and, later, Osiris, Egyptian lord of the underworld.

Phoenician deity, Ammon, originally equated with the Syrian sun god, Ba'al- Hamon, whose worship crossed into North Africa and the Mediterranean, ultimately to be conflated with the Greek high-god, Zeus, and depicted as having ram's horns. Worship of the conglomerate deity, Zeus-Ammon, began on the island of Cyrene and spread to the Greek mainland from there.

We know of the building in the second half of the fourth century BCE of a temple to Zeus-Ammon at Aphytis in the Chalcidice, an area that was annexed into the Macedonian realm under Philip II. In addition, Alexander would later associate himself and his lineage with Zeus-Ammon, including the minting of coinage that depicted the Macedonian king with the god's most prominent attribute, ram's horns. But even the attribute of the ram horns is problematic because New Kingdom pharaohs like Thutmoses III, Amenhotep III and Ramses II were depicted with ram's horns after the defeat of the Hyksos and the ritual unification of the Egyptian king with the now conflated sun god Amun-Ra (cf. Thutmoses III depicted wearing the ram's horn crown at the mortuary complex of Hatshepsut at Deir el-Bahri in Thebes).

Regardless of the original identity of the god of the shrine, which dates to the tenth century BCE, Alexander very likely made no distinction between

In the Footsteps of Perseus and Heracles

'Alexander longed to equal the fame of Perseus and Heracles; the blood of both flowed in his veins, and just as legend traced their descent from Zeus, so he, too, had a feeling that in some way he was descended from Ammon.' (Arrian III.3) Alexander could claim descent and kinship with Perseus not only through Perseus' mother, Danae, daughter of the Argive king, Acrisius, but because his ancestor on his father's side, Heracles, was the stepson of Amphitryon, the grandson of Perseus.

Syrio-Phoenician *Ammon* and Theban *Amun*, and he almost certainly equated the deity with the Zeus-Ammon, with whom he was probably already familiar, whose worship had previously been established in Northern Greece. Alexander's curiosity was no doubt further peaked about the oasis by the rumour that his ancestors Heracles and Perseus had crossed the desert and visited there. Alexander followed not only in the footsteps of divine ancestors, but celebrated Greek generals, like the Athenian Cimon and Spartan Lysander, who

Facing page: Ruins of the Temple of Ammon at Siwah. The oasis shows evidence of settlement as early as the tenth millennium BCE. Its buildings were constructed primarily of mud brick.

Above: Silver tetradrachm depicting Alexander with the ram horns of Zeus-Ammon, minted under Lysimachus, c. 305 BCE.

famously consulted the Siwah oracle, as well. Lastly, the Macedonian king almost certainly knew of the legend that Cyrus' son, Cambyses, the second Great King of Achaemenid Persia, had long ago lost an entire army in a sand storm en route to Siwah. (Herodotus II.25.3–26, Plutarch, *Alexander* XXVI.11–12). Whereas the harsh desert thwarted Cambyses' attempt to consult the oracle, Alexander would seek to prove that in all things he could outdo the Great Kings.

The 'Son of the God'?

The expedition to Siwah crossed 322km (200 miles) of arid desert in four days. Grain and water would have been difficult or impossible to obtain along the march through the wilderness. The fact was probably known to Alexander, and likely made for a difficult march, with men and beasts loaded down with provisions. When Alexander arrived at the oasis, he hurried to the site of the temple, where the senior priest greeted him, perhaps through an interpreter (as it is unlikely that a Libyan priest spoke Greek), as 'son of the God' (*pai dios*). That, at least, is what Alexander heard. But the Greek word for child, *paidion*, is remarkably similar and, if the priest of Siwah spoke broken Greek, Alexander's interpretation of the greeting may have been based on the priest's mispronunciation. The priest may have simply intended his greeting to be something along the line of, 'My child …'. It is impossible to say with certainty. Despite the priest's enigmatic greeting, the question Alexander put to the oracle was straightforward indeed: 'Tell me if you will give me the rule of the whole earth' (Diodorus Siculus XVII.51). Diodorus, Curtius and Plutarch all report that the priest answered in the affirmative. Arrian simply tells us that the priest first took Alexander on a tour of the site, during which Alexander 'received (or so he said) the answer which his heart desired' (Arrian III.4).

Let us consider that *if,* upon his arrival at the Siwah shrine, the priest hailed Alexander as 'son of the God', he simply acknowledged the Macedonian king as the legitimate pharaoh and thus, the son of Amun-Ra, just like every pharaoh before him. This is significant. For the Egyptian pharaoh was the one man in the world who could rightfully claim to have two fathers, one mortal (his human father) and one divine, Amun-Ra, who coupled in mystical union with his mother, perhaps not unlike Olympias and her snake (or thunderbolt). Conceivably, it was this very concept that the priest explained to Alexander during their tour of the grounds, which ostensibly included the temple's inner shrine, and *this* fact, the revelation of his divine parentage, fostered in him by his mother, that was now, at last, confirmed by a seemingly unbiased source. After Siwah, Alexander had his immortal parent, like Perseus, Heracles and Achilles before him. He needed not even discard Philip to get him.

But one divine parent does not a god make. Alexander knew this. And Diodorus puts in the priest's mouth the very sentiment that Alexander had carried with him since childhood: 'The proof of his divine birth will reside in the greatness of his *deeds*' (Diodorus Siculus XVII.51.2). Alexander believed that only *arete* might afford him the right to ascend to the ranks of the divine. In this, he followed heroic examples. Still, there was more to do. After Siwah, Alexander might have thought himself on his way to becoming a god, but he was too keen a student of his heroic forebears to think he had already achieved divinity. And so he pressed on, following faithfully in their footsteps and, hopefully, beyond them.

After his productive visit to Siwah, Alexander returned to Memphis where he made a grandiose sacrifice to Zeus the King, the very god whose Libyan manifestation (Ammon) he may now have believed to have been his divine father. Thereafter, he held a parade of his troops, which he followed up with games and literary contests. In the midst of the celebrations, he was joined by a force of 400 Greek mercenaries, sent by Antipater and commanded by Menidas, and a fresh contingent of 500 Thracian cavalry. Arrian tells us that Alexander was 'deeply impressed by Egypt', and one can imagine it might have played a pivotal role in his long term plans if he had lived to realize them (Arrian III.6). Before departing, he appointed two native Egyptians,

Right: The army of Cambyses II, son of Cyrus the Great, is lost in a sandstorm on the desert road to Siwah.

The God of Siwah

'The image of the god is encrusted with emeralds and other precious stones, and answers those who consult the oracle in a quite peculiar fashion. It is carried about upon a golden boat by eighty priests, and these, with the god on their shoulders, go without their own volition wherever the god directs their path. A multitude of girls and women follows them singing paeans as they go and praising the god in a traditional hymn.' (Diodorus Siculus XVII.50)

When considering the identity of the Siwan Ammon/Amun, remember that the non-Egyptian rulers of the Valley of the Nile from the eighteenth to the sixteenth centuries BCE, the Hyksos, are described by contemporaries as chieftains from Syria and Canaan with ties to Byblos on the Phoenician coast. The Hyksos, with their Ammon/Ba'al Hamon, entered the land of Amun, and in the centuries during their domination of Egypt, and thereafter, before the arrival of Alexander, the two deities may have become inextricably intertwined.

Doloaspis and Petisis, as governors of Upper and Lower Egypt, respectively. Although, as Petisis declined his appointment, the whole of Egypt's civil government fell to Doloaspis. Alexander further placed two members of the Companions over military garrisons at Memphis and Pelusium.

Darius' Terms Refused

In the Spring of 331 BCE, Alexander left Memphis and returned to Tyre. There he again made

Facing page: Temple of the Oracle of Ammon, Siwah, dating from the sixth century BCE.

sacrifice to Melqart, and was treated to a grand celebration by his Cypriot allies, who had hired for his amusement the most famous actors of the day, Athenodorus and Thessalus, to lead a grand spate of dramatic competitions that included dithyrambic choruses and tragedies, with Alexander himself acting as judge. While at Tyre, tragedy

Right: The long-reigning pharaoh, Thutmoses III (r. 1479–1425 BCE), is depicted wearing the ram's horn crown. Relief sculpture from Hatshepsut's temple, Luxor, Egypt.

struck as one of Parmenion's sons died in a boating accident. In addition, Agis III of Sparta and his brother, Agesilaus, had won over the island of Crete to their anti-Macedonian faction. Now in open rebellion, the Spartans seemed poised to use the large island as a launching pad to attempt to foment Macedonian opposition throughout the Aegean.

Alexander dispatched 100 Cypriot and Phoenician triremes to deal with the troublemakers. Otherwise, during his three-month stay at Tyre, he would receive delegations, host celebrations and begin preparations to face Darius, who had mustered an even larger army than the one he brought to Issus, at Babylon. When at last he left Tyre, Alexander made his old friend and former treasurer-general of the Macedonian army, Harpalus, satrap of Syria and marched east beyond the Syrian borders. The appointment of Harpalus suggests two things: the area was rich in resources and an important commercial and trade zone and Harpalus was a man with financial expertise, easily capable of overseeing the collection of taxes and tribute. Secondly, the area had profound strategic significance: the Syrian coast connected Asia Minor with Egypt and contained cities, like Tyre, that could harbour a significant naval presence. As such, Alexander appointed a long-time trusted colleague to ensure the continued security of the region.

By late summer, Alexander had reached Thapsacus on the Euphrates. An advance force of engineers had begun construction of two large bridges to span the river by the time of Alexander's arrival. Their work had not yet been completed. The Persian satrap of Mesopotamia, Mazaeus, was stationed on the opposite side of the river and periodically harassed the engineers. His real mission, however, seems to have been to report on Alexander's approach, for when Mazaeus spied Alexander and the main force of the Macedonian army, he withdrew immediately. The bridgework

Below: Alexander's engineering feats may have included devising an early prototype of the diving bell. Here, a medieval manuscript illustration depicts Alexander using a diving bell to see underwater at Tyre.

Harpalus, the Spy?

Scurrilous stories about Harpalus had circulated that, not long before Issus, he had defected from the king, prodded to do so by an embittered and estranged uncle of Alexander's named, Tauriscus. As Harpalus seems to have spent most of the period of his time away from the Macedonian army, not in Northern Greece, but in the Megarid, most scholars think Harpalus' 'defection' was a cover concocted by Alexander and his childhood friend that would allow Harpalus to conduct intelligence operations back in Greece. It is hard to believe indeed that the savvy Alexander would have given a traitor, not only a second chance but administrative control of a region as critical as Syria.

was finished forthwith and Alexander crossed the Euphrates unobstructed.

It may have been here, or slightly earlier, that Alexander received one last letter from Darius, offering him all the territory west of the Euphrates, 30,000 talents of silver, a treaty of alliance and the hand of his eldest daughter, Stateira, in marriage, in exchange for the cessation of hostilities between Macedon and Persia. Alexander is reported to have called together his chief commanders to discuss Darius' offer. Although he urged all in attendance to speak their minds, only the old general, Parmenion, dared to venture an opinion:

'If I were Alexander, I would accept what was offered and make a treaty'. Alexander responded, 'If I were Parmenion, so would I' (Diodorus Siculus XVII.54). After a stirring speech in which he told his men that he preferred glory to the gifts extended him by the Great King, he declared to the Persian envoys awaiting his answer that, just as two suns could not inhabit the same heaven, two kings could not rule the same earth. If Darius still wished to rule, Alexander went on, he would have to earn the right to do so on the battlefield.

The Battle of Gaugamela

In October of 331 BCE, the armies of Macedon and Achaemenid Persia would meet for the last time, on a dusty plain near the village of Gaugamela, east of the legendary city of Nineveh, the once-proud capital of the Assyrian Empire. This time Darius was determined that battlefield geography would favour him, his once-again superior numbers, and, especially, his deadly scythed chariots, armed with razor-sharp 1m (3ft) long blades, designed, quite literally, to cut through opposing infantry. We are told that Darius went so far as to grade and tamp down the terrain to create an optimal fighting surface for his 200 chariots. The Great King even engaged 15 Indian war elephants for the occasion (Arrian III.8).

Alexander's army descended a ridge overlooking the plain of Gaugamela on the afternoon of 30 September. Here, for the first time, the king caught sight of the Persian army, having already assumed a defensive posture, roughly 6.5km (four miles) away. Parmenion advised caution and a careful reconnaissance of the area, perhaps fearing that the Persians had set pit traps or other unseen obstacles on the battlefield. Although Alexander was, no doubt, eager for a decisive victory over the Great King, he heeded Parmenion's advice and rode out with a scouting party to inspect the terrain. Night fell as the king returned to the main force. Alexander summoned his senior officers to council in his tent. Some sources state that, here, Parmenion advised a night attack, arguing that the Persians would not expect it and that the surprise would cause alarm in the Persian ranks and help to compensate for the Macedonians' inferior numbers. Alexander is said to have dismissed the suggestion outright, 'I will not demean myself by stealing victory like a thief', was his reply (Arrian III.10). He then adjourned the council and ordered his men to eat and rest. On the other side of the battle lines, Darius, wary that Alexander might, in fact, attack in darkness precisely as Parmenion had counselled, ordered his men to remain vigilant and maintain their battle formations.

On the morning of 1 October, Alexander slept so soundly that Parmenion was forced to call the troops to battle order. When the king's trusted commanders, growing concerned, entered his tent and woke him, Alexander responded nonchalantly that the battle had already been won. After all, the Persians had not slept, while Alexander and his men were fresh and well-rested. But Persia's troops would not, at least in large part, fight like bleary-eyed, exhausted men.

Facing page: Alexander and his army, with quite medieval-looking and anachronistic armour and weaponry (save the ever-present *sarissa*), are depicted crossing the Tigris and Euphrates rivers. Illustration from a fifteenth-century French manuscript.

Right: Alexander (on right) looks on as a priest pours libations the night before the Battle of Gaugamela.

The preliminary formation saw Alexander, in shining ceremonial armour, commanding the right wing made up of the Companion cavalry, led by the Royal Squadron under Cleitus the Black. Beside the Companions, to their left, were the shield-bearing Guard's battalions, commanded by Nicanor. Beyond the Companions on the far right were the light-armed skirmishing troops, the Agrianians and archers, and a contingent of Greek mercenaries. The *sarissa*-wielding phalanx occupied the centre. On the left were the Thracian and Thessalian horse and other Greek allied cavalry under the leadership of Parmenion. Finally, stationed behind the main force was a second line of infantry, made up of auxiliaries from Greece, the Balkans and mercenary troops not employed elsewhere. On each flank, Alexander had his wings hang back (in echelon formation) to avoid the possibility that the enemy's superior numbers would allow them to envelop the smaller Macedonian force.

As usual, the particulars of the battle that ensued differ among the sources. This, coupled with the thick, blinding dust cloud thrown into the air by the hooves of cavalry horses on the dry, sun-scorched earth that likely made the details of the battle difficult to discern, even for the men who fought in it, render the precise chronology of events impossible to retrieve. What we can say is that the Persians attempted, and apparently succeeded, in conducting a massive encircling manoeuvre, outflanking Alexander on his right. Darius, eager to unleash his scythed chariots, knew that these weapons would become useless with the Macedonian cavalry upon them. As such, he needed to keep the Macedonian right at bay until he could successfully launch his chariots. The cavalry battle that ensued on the right, although fierce, may have played directly into Alexander's hands, and, in fact, some scholars argue that Alexander lured Darius into the outflanking manoeuver in order to force a gap in the Persian lines near the centre that Alexander could then exploit with his cavalry wedge. As at Issus, Darius himself occupied the Persian

centre and Alexander surely sought to capture or kill him quickly by means of a well-timed cavalry charge.

The whole of the Macedonian line began to tilt right to compensate for the Persian numbers attempting to envelop the Macedonians' right flank. This, in turn, created a gap in the Macedonian lines, isolating Parmenion and his troops on the left, who were now forced to engage a much larger number of the enemy. Perhaps sensing that he had gained the upper hand, Darius now released his scythed chariots. The gambit failed miserably. A number of the chariots were intercepted by the missiles of the Agrianians and javelin-throwing skirmishers, who hurled their weapons and proceeded to seize the reins of chariots and drag their drivers to the ground. The chariots that did reach the Macedonian lines did so to no effect whatsoever, for when they approached, the troops, as they had been ordered to do beforehand, deliberately broke formation and allowed the vehicles to pass through benignly, their steely scythes neutralized by the Macedonians' acute combination of agility and discipline.

Cavalry Battle

If the cavalry battle on the right was evenly matched, Parmenion was getting the worst of it on the left, with Mazaeus, commander of the Persian right, using his horses and a few chariots to great effect to take advantage of what gaps had been created in the Macedonian lines. But old Parmenion held firm, refusing to buckle, and those of Mazaeus' horsemen who felt cavalier enough to ride ahead and pillage Alexander's camp had underestimated the resolve of the grizzled Macedonian general.

Finally, on the right, Alexander found his opening, when the Great King's Bactrian units, under the command of Bessus, were moved far enough to their left to create a gap that Alexander spotted instantly. He now took his place at the head of the wedge, the Royal Squadron riding behind him. The remaining Companions, pushing forward in oblique formation, were joined on their left by the phalanx, raising their terrifying war cry.

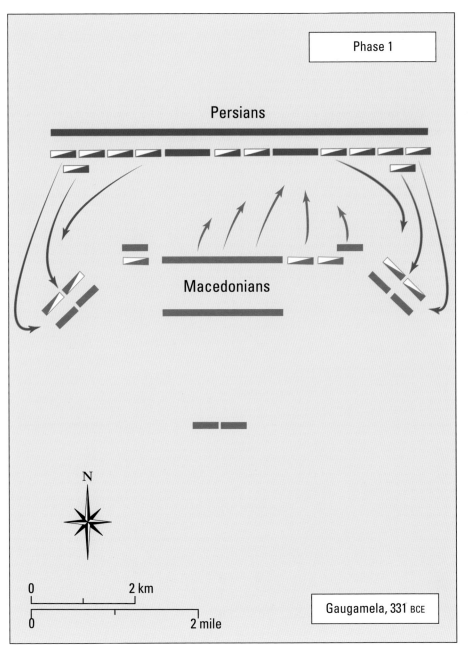

Phase 1

Persians

Macedonians

N

0		2 km

0		2 mile

Gaugamela, 331 BCE

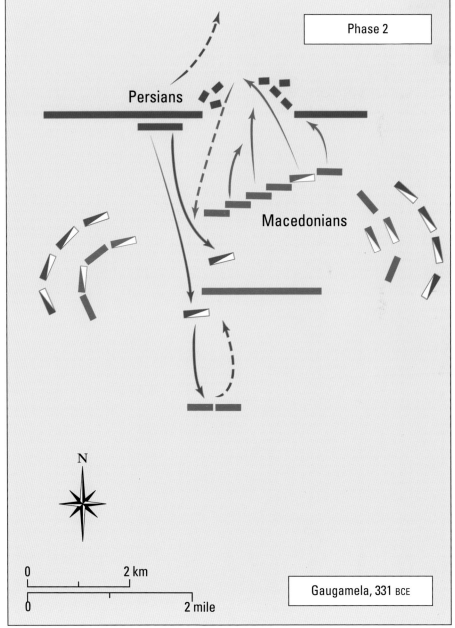

Phase 2

Persians

Macedonians

N

0		2 km

0		2 mile

Gaugamela, 331 BCE

Above: Alexander's dusty victory, and final engagement against Darius III, on the plain of Gaugamela.

Facing page: 'The Battle of Arbela (Battle of Gaugamela)' by J. Castillo (1737–1793). Based on a painting by Pietro da Cortona (San Fernando Royal Academy Museum, Madrid).

Alexander's ingenious use of the phalanx to create a giant combination wedge of infantry and cavalry forced the Persian centre to focus its energies on the Macedonian foot and not their lethal cavalry. Since the phalanx abandoned its traditional position to join Alexander's massive wedge, the auxiliaries he had positioned as second-line infantry came to play a critical role, not only in continuing to occupy the Persian centre as the wedge advanced, but in helping to support the struggling Macedonian left. The Persian centre, facing the advancing phalanx, the second-line infantry and the oncoming Macedonian

horse, became disoriented and weakened about the time Alexander slammed into it. As the Companions pressed in toward the heart of the Persian centre, and the Great King himself, Darius, fearing that he was about to be cut off and isolated, broke and ran.

As at Issus, Alexander's pursuit of Darius was delayed, this time both by the colossal cloud of dust that made visibility problematic and by reports that the beleaguered Macedonian left was in desperate need of reinforcements. The battle may have been won, but the fighting was not yet over. When the Companions turned and met the formidable forces on the Persian right, they met the stiffest resistance of the day and 60 Companions fell. Alexander's dear friend, Hephaestion, was wounded.

At last, with the forces on the Persian right beaten back, Alexander had his decisive, definitive victory. Much to his frustration, however, he still did not have Darius, and he was loathe to pursue him, immediately at least, in the wake of the day's hard-fought, dust-choked struggle. He preferred to give his men time to rest, to recover and to mourn the losses of their kinsmen. But, if one story is true, dead or alive, prisoner or fugitive, Alexander had nothing more to fear from the former Great King, for when Mazaeus' troops had pillaged Alexander's camp, they found the queen mother, Sisygambis, Alexander's well-treated hostage. They begged her to come with them, pledging to return her to her son. She refused, desiring instead to remain with Alexander. It seems that even Darius' mother could see the writing on the wall.

The Rewards and Costs of Conquest

At midnight on 2 October 331 BCE, Alexander's burning desire to capture Darius became too great to resist and he struck out across the desert, riding some 120km (75 miles) through the night, arriving at the city of Arbela at dawn.

H e hoped to find the former Great King hiding there, but, by the time he entered the city, Darius was already gone. He had left behind a considerable war chest, 4000 talents in coin and a significant portion of his baggage train. Soon Alexander and his intelligence officers were able

Facing page: Alexander's reception at Babylon was an extravagant one. The king's arrival is depicted here in seventeenth-century French painter Charles Le Brun's 'The Entry of Alexander into Babylon'.

Right: Replica of the 'Tyrannicides', Harmodius and Aristogeiton, by Antenor. The two men assassinated the Pisistratid Tyrant, Hipparchus, in 514 BCE, beginning a chain of events that led to the emergence of Athenian democracy under Cleisthenes (508/507 BCE).

to cobble together the particulars of Darius' escape. Alexander had predicted correctly that the defeated Great King would flee to Arbela to be joined there by Bessus and the surviving members of his Bactrian cavalry and some Greek mercenaries. But Darius' sojourn in Arbela was short-lived.

After a brief speech before the remnants of his army and probably a war council with Bessus and other remaining generals, Darius would set out for Media by way of the treacherous mountains of Armenia. His rationale was that the mountain passes would be difficult for Alexander and his large army to navigate, and anyway, Alexander would surely first set his sights on the great cities of Susa and Babylon. The roads to these manifest prizes of the Persian

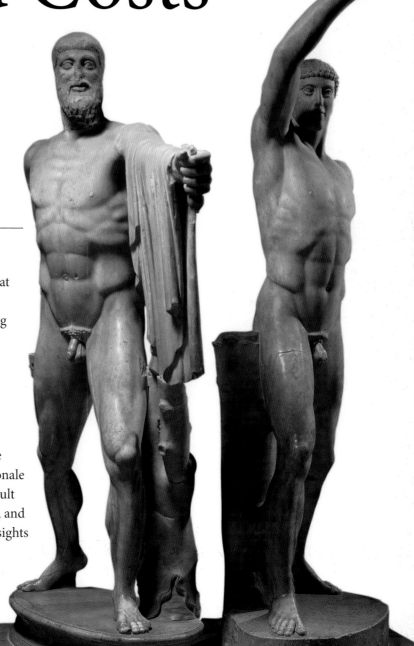

**Above: 'Entry of Alexander the Great into Babylon',
by Austrian Rococo painter Johann Georg Platzer
(1704–1761).**

who had harried Parmenion's forces at Gaugamela, had, after the battle, made haste to Babylon to take command of the garrison there. When Alexander arrived, it was Mazaeus and his sons who greeted him. They were clad in suppliants' clothing and they threw themselves on the ground before Alexander in a distinctly Persian gesture of ritual obeisance, *proskynesis*. In doing so, they acknowledged Alexander as the new Great King of Persia.

Thereafter, the Babylonians, like the Egyptians before them, a proud people with a storied past, threw open the gates of their city and enthusiastically celebrated the arrival of their new king. As he walked the garlanded, flower-strewn streets of the city, Alexander was presented with gifts of every kind. The city's treasurer, Bagophanes, lavished him with fine horses and even, so we are told, lions and leopards, whose cages thereafter joined the king's triumphal procession.

Singers and musicians, who typically sang paeans in praise of Persia's Great King, lined the streets and lifted their voices in praise of Alexander. With this grandiose welcome and the many other attractions that Babylon had to offer, from the finest food and drink to the most beautiful male and female courtesans to the spectacular monuments that testified to the city's ancient pedigree, it is little wonder that Alexander chose to remain with his army in Babylon for 34 days.

The next stop on Alexander's itinerary was Susa, Persia's administrative capital. Leaving Babylon, he appointed his former adversary, Mazaeus, satrap, a gesture of gratitude for the former Persian

heartland, with their embarrassment of riches, were easily negotiable, even for a great army with a substantial baggage train.

Babylon and Beyond

Babylon lay 462km (287 miles) from Arbela. As Darius guessed, Alexander made for the great city rather than continue to pursue the former Persian king into the mountain wastes of Media. Mazaeus,

A Grand Babylonian Welcome

'A large number of Babylonians had taken up a position on the walls, eager to have a view of their new king, but most went out to meet him, including the man in charge of the citadel and royal treasury, Bagophanes. Not to be outdone by Mazaeus in paying his respects to Alexander, Bagophanes had carpeted the whole road with flowers and garlands and set up at intervals on both sides silver altars heaped not just with frankincense but with all manner of perfumes. Following were his gifts – herds of cattle and horses and lions, too, and leopards carried along in cages. Next came the Magi chanting a song in their native fashion, and behind them were the Chaldaeans, then the Babylonians, represented not only by priests but also by musicians equipped with their national instrument. [The role of the latter was to sing the praises of the Persian kings, that of the Chaldaeans to reveal astronomical movements and regular seasonal changes.] At the rear came the Babylonian cavalry, their equipment and that of the horses suggesting extravagance rather than majesty.

'Surrounded by an armed guard, the king instructed the townspeople to follow at the rear of his infantry: he then entered the city on a chariot and went into the palace.'

QUINTUS CURTIUS RUFUS, V.1.19–23

Above: 'Alexander Enters Babylon', from an eighteenth-century illustration.

Babylonian Excess: The Lurid Reputation of an Ancient Metropolis

'Alexander halted longer in this city than anywhere else, and here he undermined military discipline more than in any other place. The moral corruption there is unparalleled; its ability to stimulate and arouse unbridled passions is incomparable. Parents and husbands permit their children and wives to have sex with strangers, as long as this infamy is paid for. All over the Persian empire kings and their courtiers are fond of parties, and the Babylonians are especially addicted to wine and the excesses that go along with drunkenness. Women attend dinner parties. At first they are decently dressed, then they remove all their top-clothing and by degrees disgrace their respectability until (I beg my readers' pardon for saying it) they finally throw off their most intimate garments. This disgusting conduct is characteristic not only of courtesans but also of married women and young girls, who regard vile prostitution as "being sociable".'

Quintus Curtius Rufus, V.1.36–38

Above: Saddam Hussein's reconstruction of ancient Babylon in modern-day Iraq, with its grid-like streets. Image shot in 2003.

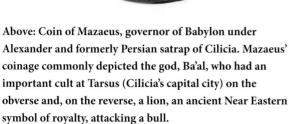

Above: Coin of Mazaeus, governor of Babylon under Alexander and formerly Persian satrap of Cilicia. Mazaeus' coinage commonly depicted the god, Ba'al, who had an important cult at Tarsus (Cilicia's capital city) on the obverse and, on the reverse, a lion, an ancient Near Eastern symbol of royalty, attacking a bull.

commander's surrender of the city. The march from Babylon to Susa was begun near the end of November and took about 20 days. Alexander now approached the very heart of the Achaemenid Empire and, as such, he could no longer portray himself as liberator. Now, he became a conqueror, leading the overthrow of a 230-year-old world empire. At Susa, Alexander entered the royal palace and treasury to find great riches, including

50,000 talents of silver and other prizes formerly possessed by the Great King. Darius' treasure trove even contained spoils that Xerxes had brought back from his sack of Athens in 480 BCE, among them monumental bronze statues of Harmodius and Aristogeiton, the revolutionary lovers who had assassinated the Greek tyrant Hipparchus. Alexander immediately ordered that the statues be returned to Athens. Hereafter, he celebrated solemn rights and sacrifices to the traditional Greek gods and held games and a torch race. Having spent perhaps two weeks at Susa, Alexander allowed the Persian, Abulites, to retain the satrapy of the region, and placed a member of the Companions in charge of the city's garrison force. He also allowed Darius' mother, Sisygambis, and the remaining members

Alexander on the (Oversized) Persian Throne

'A curious thing happened to the king when he was shown the precious objects. He seated himself upon the royal throne, which was larger than the proportion of his body. When one of the pages saw that his feet were a long way from reaching the footstool which belonged to the throne, he picked up Darius' table and placed it under the king's dangling legs. This fitted, and the king was pleased by the aptness of the boy, but a Persian eunuch standing nearby was troubled in his heart at this reminder of the changes of fortune and he wept. Alexander noticed him and asked, "What wrong have you seen that you are crying?" The eunuch replied, "Now I am your slave as formerly I was the slave of Darius. I am by nature devoted to my masters and I was grieved at seeing what was most held in honour by your predecessors now become an ignoble piece of furniture."

'The eunuch's answer reminded the king how great a change had overcome the Persian kingdom. He saw that he had committed an act of arrogance quite the reverse of his gentleness to the captives, and calling over the page who had placed the table beneath his feet ordered him to remove it.'

DIODORUS SICULUS, XVII.66

of his family to reside at Susa and provided them with tutors to teach them Greek. His next objective: Persepolis.

The Defeat of the Uxii and the Battle of the Persian Gates

Passing out of Susa's hinterland and the fertile marshes of the Pasitigris (Karun) River, Alexander entered the land of the Uxii, a confederation of unaffiliated tribesmen who controlled the mountain passes to the Persian Gates. The Uxii, who had never recognized Persian authority, sent a message to Alexander that the Great King had always paid them tribute when he desired to navigate their mountain passes. They demanded that Alexander do the same. Unwilling to yield to this ultimatum or to accept the independence of the Uxii, Alexander devised a clever ruse whereby he told the mountain chieftains that he would meet them at the pass with their requested tribute the following day.

That night, he led a force consisting of members of his royal bodyguard, the Guards battalions and a number of other troops on a raid of the Uxian villages, wherein he killed a number of tribespeople and took considerable plunder. While the Uxii were thus occupied, Alexander sent Craterus and a contingent of Macedonian infantry ahead to secure the pass before dawn broke the next morning. With the mountain pass in hand and the Uxian

Right: The Elamite settlement ruins in Susa (now Shush) Iran, pre-dating the rise of Cyrus (r. 559–530 BCE) and the Achaemenids.

villages in disarray, the hill tribes had no choice but to surrender to Alexander, at which point he demanded a significant annual levy of livestock and draft animals. The Uxians, being herdsmen, were well known in the region for their prime horses and sheep, and, thereafter, Alexander would make good use of their animals in exchange for allowing them to remain in their homes and villages undisturbed.

Now, Alexander advanced to the Persian Gates, the pass through the Zagros mountains that lead to Persepolis, where he faced serious opposition from the satrap of Persis, Ariobarzanes, who had packed the gorge with 25,000 men, erected a wall across the pass at its narrowest point and stationed men to command the heights above the narrow defile. Alexander's first inclination, of course, was to take up Ariobarzanes' challenge by way of a bold frontal assault. But the Macedonians were repulsed and took heavy losses, inflicted by the missiles that rained down from the heights. Regrouping, Alexander made use of intelligence provided by local herdsmen to circumnavigate the pass and fall upon Ariobarzanes' position from the rear with the Guards battalions, an infantry battalion commanded by Perdiccas, a contingent of the light-armed skirmishers, the Agrianians and archers, the Royal Squadron of the Companions and two more cavalry squadrons.

As Alexander's forces fell upon the enemy, trumpets blaring, Craterus led an assault on the Persian defences from the other side of the gorge. Meanwhile, Philotas and Amyntas, son of Andromenes, were given the charge of scaling the heights with a contingent tasked to take out the Persian troops who commanded the hilltops. This coordinated attack succeeded in surrounding Ariobarzanes' forces on all sides. Although Ariobarzanes and a few cavalry managed to escape into the hills, the Persian Gates belonged to Alexander.

The Burning of Persepolis

Alexander probably reached Persepolis in early February 330 BCE. The majestic city, founded by Darius I 'the Great' and completed by his son Xerxes, was the very embodiment of the Achaemenids' imperial achievement. It was their empire's ritual and ceremonial capital, a grandiose military training site and a summer residence for the kings replete with glorious reception halls, lavish royal living quarters and gorgeous monumental architecture and artistry, all of which was entered via Xerxes' 'Gate of All Lands', which proclaimed the colossal city a world capital, welcoming of all peoples. It was during his stay at Persepolis that

Right: Perdiccas, d. 321 BCE, Macedonian general and life-long friend of Alexander. Perdiccas received Alexander's signet ring (the symbol of his kingship) upon his death and declared his intention to rule as regent until Alexander's infant son (by Roxane) came of age.

Left: The ancient Persian Gates, in the mountain pass today known as Tang-e Meyran, part of the Zagros mountains.

Facing page: Thais suggests that Alexander burn Persepolis, ceremonial capitol of Achaemenid Persia, in 331 BCE.

Alexander committed what history would judge to be one of the most significant atrocities of his career, the burning of Xerxes' magnificent palace and much of the city's royal quarter in the wake of a drinking party that had seemingly spiralled out of hand. Our sources claim that the conflagration was instigated by an Athenian courtesan, Thais, who was soon to become the mistress of Ptolemy, son of Lagus. Thais had suggested that Alexander burn the palace as revenge for the sacrilege Xerxes had wrought upon Athens so many years ago.

Flush with drink, Alexander and his commanders, Parmenion excepted, thought this a splendid idea. They seized torches and began setting fire to the great building. Parmenion, attempting to bring Alexander to his senses, asked why the king would stupidly set fire to his own property, but, with the palace's cedar-wood ceiling already aflame, the damage had been done and, soon, a debauched surfeit of destruction ensued. A significant portion of the army joined the commanders in the destructive revelry, wherein the palace was gutted and priceless treasures smashed. In the cold light of the following day, Alexander seems to have regretted his decision to engage in such senseless vandalism. It would not be the last time that he would act in drunken haste and mourn the folly of his indiscretion.

Facing page: A modern depiction of the burning of
Persepolis by Alexander and his men.

The Death of Darius

At some point between Alexander's return to Tyre
in 331 BCE and his victory at Gaugamela in October
of that same year, Darius' wife, Stateira, had died
in childbirth. Since she had been captured after
the Battle of Issus in November 333 BCE, the child
she carried certainly did not belong to Darius.
We cannot say definitively that the child was
Alexander's either, but it certainly strains credulity
to imagine that anyone would have been granted
access to the Persian queen without Alexander's
knowledge and permission.

News of Stateira's death and the manner of it may
have only just reached Darius, who was regrouping
and rebuilding his forces at Ecbatana in Media, and
he may have become despondent or enraged. Either
way, he was judged by his most senior remaining
general, the cavalry commander Bessus, to be unfit
to lead. As such, Bessus relieved the king and, either
out of respect or black humour, he bound his new
prisoner in gold chains and threw him in the back
of a wagon, determined to run for the time being
rather than face Alexander again.

Having learned of Darius' location, Alexander
made for Ecbatana with some 17,000 of his most
mobile troops by way of the Deh Bid Pass, 2438.5m
(8000ft) above sea level. Even in late March, when
Alexander would have crossed the pass, he would
have encountered ice and snow drifts that would
have made the trek particularly cruel. Curtius
describes in gloomy, near-apocalyptic detail the
difficulties Alexander's men faced as they travelled
toward Ecbatana in hopes of capturing the fugitive
former king. The road from Persepolis to Ecbatana
stretched for 827km (514 miles), much of it
through desolate mountain wilderness. Whatever
amusements Alexander's men had enjoyed in
Babylon and Persepolis, they would have found little

Below: 'The Death of Stateira, Wife of Darius', by Louis Jean
Francois Lagrenée (1725–1805), oil on canvas.

The Frozen Road to Ecbatana

'They had reached a road covered with permanent snow which was frozen hard by the intense cold. The desolation of the terrain and the trackless wilderness terrified the exhausted soldiers, who thought they were looking at the limits of the world. They gazed in astonishment at the total desolation with no sign of human cultivation, and they clamoured to go back before daylight and sky also came to an end. The king refrained from reproaching them for their fear instead he jumped from his horse and proceeded to make his way on foot through the snow and hard-packed ice. His friends were ashamed not to follow him, and the feeling spread to his officers, and, finally, the men. The king was the first to clear a way for himself, using an axe to break the ice, and then the others followed his example.'

QUINTUS CURTIUS RUFUS, V.6.13–14

Right: Tappe-e Hekmatane, Ecbatana archaeological site, modern Hamadan, Iran.

pleasure in the gruelling march through Media in search of Persia's vanquished king.

Alexander's weary men at last reached Ecbatana to find Darius gone or dragged away by the usurper Bessus, who had now claimed for himself the title of Great King. The pretender king and his party, having learned that Alexander was gaining on them, decided to ditch the heavy wagon that held Darius in order to speed up their flight. Bessus ordered Darius to mount a horse, but Darius refused, asserting that he would not accompany traitors any further. Although, as Arrian confirms, Bessus would have preferred to keep Darius alive in the event that Alexander overtook him and he needed a bargaining chip, he could not endure the former king's insults: a true king is not shamed before the men he seeks to lead. And so the life of Darius came to a sad end at the points of javelins and the hands of a usurper.

Just beyond the Caspian Gates, not far from Hecatompylos, Alexander finally secured the body of Darius. The moment, on a July afternoon in 330 BCE, was a defining one, but it surely did not play out as Alexander had intended. Alexander found the wagon that had transported the former king bogged down in mud, the twisted body of Darius, still impaled with javelins, discarded like refuse in the back. Alexander's advance scouts had located the sorry scene first and found Darius still alive, gasping for breath. But Alexander would not reach the former king in time to hear his last words, which, according to Plutarch, entailed a request for water and the following: 'This is the final stroke of

Right: Alexander's scouts find the dying Darius III, in this nineteenth-century magazine illustration.

misfortune that I should accept service from you and not be able to return it, but Alexander will reward you for your kindness, and the gods will repay him for his courtesy toward my mother, and my wife, and my children. And so through you, I give him my hand.' (Plutarch, *Life of Alexander,* 43)

This speech is most likely apocryphal, as Darius' wife had died in Alexander's care, and a man who had been the Great King of Persia would hardly have bemoaned his inability to return a gesture from the sort of men he had spent his life viewing as mere servants. But Plutarch' account does point to the larger issue. With the legitimate Great King of Persia dead, there now lived no one who could truly challenge Alexander's claim to imperial authority. We are told that Alexander was moved and disgusted by the sight of Darius' body and that he took off his own cloak to cover the gruesome spectacle. He ordered, forthwith, the burial of Darius with full ceremonial honours at Persepolis, alongside his Achaemenid ancestors. And, as Darius' legitimate heir, he now committed himself to avenge his murder. The regicide Bessus now returned to Bactria, his home, to continue recruiting and urging resistance against Alexander.

Oriental Despotism?

Alexander moved ahead to Zadracarta, a town in Hyrcania, where he received a number of high-ranking Persian envoys, including the

Facing page: Alexander is depicted mourning over the body of the dead Darius.

Right: Marble statue of a wounded Amazon warrior, Roman copy of a Greek original by the celebrated sculptor, Phidias (c. 480–430 BCE).

general, Artabazus, who had fought with Darius at Gaugamela, aided him in his initial flight, and remained loyal to him even in the wake of Bessus' coup. Alexander rewarded Artabazus for his devotion to the former king by appointing him governor of Bessus' home satrapy of Bactria. Alexander also received representatives from the 1500 Greek mercenaries who had fought with Darius to the last. He told their delegates that he would accept nothing except unconditional surrender. Greek soldiers, he argued, who had fought for Persia against their own homeland were 'little better than criminals …' (Arrian, III.23). The mercenaries accepted his terms and were thereafter incorporated into the Macedonian army.

After these delegations, Alexander conducted a campaign against the Mardians, who were resisting the imposition of his rule. He began to pacify the countryside forcibly. In retaliation, a brazen group of Mardians launched a raid and stole Bucephalus. Alexander sent word to the natives through interpreters that, if the horse were not returned immediately, they would see their entire countryside 'laid waste to its furthest limits and its inhabitants slaughtered to a man' (Diodorus Siculus, XVII.76). When the Mardian natives failed to respond promptly, Alexander immediately began to carry

out his threat and soon the terrified locals had returned the horse with the costliest gifts and presents for Alexander they could muster and 50 men as suppliants to beg the king's forgiveness. With the Mardians successfully subjugated and Bucephalus recovered, Alexander travelled across Parthia to Sousia, probably along the ancient Silk Road.

It is probably here, and not in Hyrcania, as Diodorus reports, where he received an embassy led by the queen of the Amazons, Thalestris, who ruled the country between the rivers Phasis and Thermodon. When the king asked her why she had come, she replied that, having heard of Alexander's remarkable achievements, she wished him to impregnate her with a child. Flattered by her request and impressed both by her beauty and warrior-like physique, Alexander consorted with her for a fortnight, after which he lavished her with gifts and sent her on her way. Alexander now learned that Bessus was parading around Bactria calling himself the lord of Asia, that he was wearing the Persian royal diadem and that he had changed his name to Artaxerxes V.

Alexander himself had now begun to wear the diadem that marked the person of the Great King and to take on increasingly Orientalizing trappings. To see their king

adorned in Persian dress displeased some among the Macedonians, but it did not stop Alexander from assuming elements of the Persian royal wardrobe, rituals and protocol. One of those protocols was the ritual of *proskynesis*, which entailed prostrating oneself on the ground before the person of the Great King, a gesture that, for Macedonian aristocrats, was reserved for deities. To men who had always been Companions, near-equals to their king, this came as an unwelcome change.

With Alexander en route to Bactria and Bessus, he faced rebellion on a second front, from Satabarzanes, who had surrendered himself to Alexander at Sousia and had been allowed to maintain his satrapy at Areia. As he was escorted home by Anaxippus and a contingent of 40 javelinmen tasked by Alexander to oversee military affairs in the satrapy, Satabarzanes massacred his escort and revolted. Distracted from pursuing Bessus, Alexander turned south and met the rebels at Artacoana, perhaps near Herat, where he soundly defeated Satabarzanes' rebels, although the governor himself and a handful of supporters escaped Alexander's grasp.

The Conspiracy of Philotas and the Fall of Parmenion

Alexander now made his way to Phrada to regroup. There he would face an ignominious scandal that would lead to the deaths of two of his prized commanders. The details of the conspiracy that consumed Alexander's court and implicated Parmenion's eldest son, Philotas, surrounded a plot

Facing page: 'Thalestris in the court of Alexander', by Johann Georg Platzer (1704–1761).

Left: The court of Alexander, as illustrated in a Persian manuscript. Stories and legends of Alexander are a common theme in Islamic art and literature, a fact that demonstrates the sheer scope of Alexander's influence and legacy.

against Alexander's life. The prime movers in the
sordid affair seem to have been Demetrius, one
of the seven members of Alexander's elite royal
bodyguard (*somatophylakes*), who was joined by a
number of other minor accomplices, including one,
Dimnus, a member of the Companions and distant
associate of the king. When Dimnus attempted to
recruit his lover, the young Nicomachus (who may
or may not have been a male prostitute), to the plot,
Dimnus' protégé became frightened and reported
the incident to his brother, Cebalinus, an officer of
some rank. Cebalinus, in turn, approached Philotas
with the details of the conspiracy, and, fearing that
his brother could face reprisals, asked the son of
Parmenion to intervene on their family's behalf with
the king.

For whatever reason, Philotas initially did
nothing, and the following day, Cebalinus
approached Philotas once more with his request.
When Philotas again failed to approach Alexander
on Cebalinus' behalf, the latter lost faith in Philotas
and appealed to the king himself. Alexander hastily
ordered the arrest of Dimnus, who was either
killed resisting arrest or committed suicide. The
arrests of Demetrius and Philotas followed shortly
thereafter. Philotas' defence was that he had not
taken Cebalinus' claims seriously, that Cebalinus
had an overactive imagination and that his
brother, Nicomachus, was a male prostitute, whose
allegations could not be trusted. Philotas may have
been troubled by Alexander's recent experiments
with Persian court rituals, but it is hard to accept
that he played a principal role in a plot to assassinate

the king. Philotas did, however, on the verge of execution, implicate a certain Calis as Demetrius' primary accomplice. This Calis later admitted that he and Demetrius had planned the crime.

Whether or not Philotas played any role in the conspiracy, his failure to report the rumblings of it was a grave mistake. Perhaps he was disenchanted enough with Alexander that he was content to let events play out or, perhaps, he truly believed that the accusations rested on the overblown rantings of a reactionary blowhard and his prostitute brother. The whole affair troubled Alexander deeply, and he seems to have consulted his intimates, Hephaestion, Craterus and Coenus, at nearly every turn, but in the end, Alexander could not bring himself to let Philotas live, for he had betrayed the sacred trust of the king, even if merely by his silence.

One final note on the conspiracy is that Philotas' colleague, Amyntas, son of Andromenes, became implicated as well, along with his three brothers. Amyntas put up a vigorous defence and was acquitted by the same court that condemned Philotas. Executed along with Philotas, Demetrius, Calis and others named by Nicomachus, was Alexander the Lyncestian, son-in-law of Antipater, who had been the first to declare for Alexander at Philip's assassination, but had been arrested three years earlier on suspicion of conspiring with the Persians to assassinate Alexander. He had been hauled around in chains by the Macedonian army ever since.

Alexander's next move, though perhaps understandable, stands among the darkest of his career. Parmenion had been stationed at Ecbatana and to there Alexander dispatched an old friend of the veteran general, Polydamus the Thessalian, one of the Companions. Polydamus carried with him a letter signed by the king and addressed to Cleander, Sitalces and Menidas, three generals under Parmenion's command. It ordered them to put to death the man who had served the Macedonian royal house with distinction for three decades, and perhaps more, and who, for at least the past ten years, had effectively been Philip's and Alexander's right hand. There is almost no doubt in the minds of ancient or modern historians that Parmenion played no part whatever in a conspiracy to assassinate the king. In Arrian's words, '… even granting his [Parmenion's] innocence, his living on after his son's execution was already in fact a danger; for he was a man of immense prestige' (III.127). Parmenion had to die, not necessarily because of something he had done, but because of what he might do in response to Alexander's execution of his son. When Alexander decided Philotas' fate, he surely understood that he was deciding the fate of Parmenion as well. If Plutarch is to be believed,

Above: Plutarch of Chaeronea (c. 46–c. 120 CE), historian and biographer. From a sixteenth-century manuscript illustration.

Left: Alexander's army crosses the Oxus. Medieval manuscript illustration from Plutarch's *Life of Alexander*.

Facing page: Alexander's harsh punishment of the usurper, Bessus (from a nineteenth-century magazine illustration).

Antipater, when he heard of Parmenion's death remarked: 'If Parmenion plotted against Alexander, who is to be trusted? And if he did not, what is to be done?' (Plutarch, *Moralia,* 183F 1).

The Capture of Bessus

With the conspiracy and its casualties behind him, Alexander now focused his full attention on the capture of Bessus. He pursued Bessus all the way to the Oxus River. He had crossed a section of the Hindu Kush mountains to get there, another punishing march in pursuit of an elusive target. Bessus had crossed the Oxus and was hiding out in Sogdiana, under the care of the war chief, Spitamenes, who, while he had no love for the Macedonians, likewise had no desire to die at their hands for sheltering Darius' murderer. Spitamenes sent a message to Alexander that he was placing Bessus under arrest and that, if the king would send a Macedonian officer and escort to a particular spot, they would find Bessus under guard to be handed over to them forthwith.

Ptolemy, son of Lagus, now commander of the royal bodyguard with Demetrius having been executed, was chosen to lead the mission. The force that accompanied him was hardly a traditional escort. It may have comprised as many as 1600 cavalry and 4000 infantry. Ptolemy was directed to

a remote location north of the river, where he found Bessus as Spitamenes had promised. Alexander instructed Ptolemy to strip Bessus naked, fit him with a wooden collar and drag him back along the road. When the prisoner approached Alexander's camp, the king met him in the Persian royal chariot, wearing the diadem that Bessus had seized for himself, a powerful symbolic gesture that drove home with utmost clarity the true identity of Persia's Great King.

Claiming himself the avenger of Darius' murder, Alexander dealt with Bessus harshly, first cutting off his nose and ears, a distinctly Persian punishment inflicted upon traitors. Our sources do not agree on the ultimate manner of Bessus' death. However it came, either by crucifixion, brutal torture and decapitation, or by being ripped in half, Alexander would have seen it as fitting punishment for a man who would betray and murder his king. In addition to capturing Bessus at the Oxus, Alexander's forces secured the territory immediately north of the river and campaigned in and around Maracanda, setting up a Macedonian garrison there.

Alexander may have hoped that the capture and execution of Bessus meant the end of serious opposition to his rule. But the Sogdian warlord Spitamenes had played a clever hand, turning over the usurper and lulling Alexander into a false sense of security. And so, in late summer or early autumn

Facing page: Relief of Sogdians, the Apadana, frieze showing Sogdian delegates bringing tribute to the Great King. Persepolis (Iran).

329 BCE, Alexander called the local barons of Sogdiana and Bactria and other regional leaders to a summit at Bactra in hopes of presenting himself as the legitimate successor of Darius. Spitamenes, admired and feared by the local tribes, advised them against meeting with or negotiating with Alexander, who, not unlike Bessus, was a mere usurper of the Great King's throne. Maybe here, in anticipation of fighting a potential guerrilla war against Spitamenes and his allies, Alexander reorganized elements of his army, beginning with the Companions, which he now divided into about six *hipparchies*, larger contingents than the former *ilai*, which had originally contained 200 or 300 men. The *hipparchs*, leaders of these formidable cavalry contingents, were comprised of Alexander's closest and most trusted generals – with the exception of Craterus, who after Parmenion's death became supreme commander of the Macedonian infantry. Among the *hipparchs* were Hephaestion, Ptolemy, Perdiccas and Leonnatus.

Now, or very shortly hereafter, also emerge the Silver Shields (*Argyraspides*), an upgraded version of the Guards battalions, who now wore shining silver plated armour to go along with their heavy convex shields from which they derived their name. These troops had always been more mobile than the Macedonian infantry phalanx and now they seem to have become an elite moveable fighting force whose look was meant to make as grand an impression as its skill. Perhaps Alexander already anticipated using the Guards in a different way, more like a heavy-armed skirmishing force, which might prove

Above: The head of the rebel, Spitamenes, is presented to Alexander. Seventeenth-century manuscript illustration of Curtius' *History of Alexander* (8.3).

especially useful on the difficult terrain of Sogdiana and Bactria.

The Sogdian Rock

By 328 BCE, Spitamenes was bold enough to attack the Macedonian garrison at Maracanda, in Sogdiana. When Alexander left the city of Bactra to provide Maracanda with reinforcements, Spitamenes withdrew and began launching raids into Bactria instead. Spitamenes mustered an army formidable enough to make a play for the city of Bactra whose defence Alexander had left to Artabazus. The Persian satrap and Macedonian ally successfully thwarted Spitamenes' attempt to do violence to Bactria's capital. From Maracanda, Alexander ultimately sent forces under Craterus and Coenus to chase the Sogdian warlord out of Bactria. Whether or not Spitamenes represented a serious threat to Alexander, he was certainly a considerable headache. Shortly after a defeat at the hands of Coenus late in 328 BCE, Spitamenes was killed by his wife, who sent his head to Alexander as a gesture of capitulation and petition for the cessation of hostilities.

While north of the Oxus, Alexander's attentions were drawn to the seemingly impregnable fortress of the Sogdian Rock, the last stronghold of Sogdian resistance. The towering fortification was commanded by a recalcitrant sympathizer of Spitamenes and Oxyartes, the Bactrian (who had

Left: Detail from a sixteenth-century fresco, 'The Marriage of Alexander and Roxane', by G. A. Bazzi (Sodoma) in the Villa Farnesina.

Ascending the Sogdian Rock

'There were some 300 men who in previous sieges had experience in rock climbing. These now assembled. They had provided themselves with small iron tent pegs, which they proposed to drive into the snow, where it was frozen hard, or into any bit of bare earth they might come across, and they had attached to the pegs small flaxen lines. The party set off under cover of darkness to the steepest part of the rock face, which they knew was least likely to be guarded; then, driving their pegs either into bare ground or into such patches of snow as seemed most likely to hold under the strain, they hauled themselves up, wherever each could find a way. About thirty lost their lives during the ascent – falling in various places in the snow, their bodies were never recovered for burial – but the rest reached the top as dawn was breaking and the summit of the Rock was theirs. Then, in accordance with Alexander's orders, they signalled their success to the troops below by waving bits of linen, and Alexander sent a crier to shout the news to the enemy's advance posts that they might now surrender without further delay, as the men with wings had been found and were already in possession of the summit.'

ARRIAN, IV.19.

Above: Remains of an ancient Sogdian citadel, possibly the so-called 'Sogdian Rock'. Penjikent, Tajikistan.

likewise refused to submit to Alexander). This
Ariamazes, commander of the great rock, had given
refuge to Oxyartes' wife and daughters and the
remaining hold-outs against the king. The defenders
of the fortress all but dared Alexander to come and
get them, suggesting that to seize the rock would
require 'soldiers with wings' (Arrian, IV.19). The
dual reward of taking the last bastion of Sogdian
opposition and accomplishing a feat that men
deemed impossible would certainly have excited
Alexander. To that end, he pledged significant
monetary rewards to the first men who could scale
the rock, 12 talents to the first man up, 11 to the
second, 10 to the third and so on all the way to the
twelfth man.

Arrian does not relate the height of the rock,
although Curtius (VII.11) claims that it rose some
5480m (18,000ft) high, a clear exaggeration. It is
not unusual for Sogdian peaks to reach heights of
6096m (20,000 feet), but scaling a cliff wall of that
magnitude would surely have been beyond the
reach even of the great Alexander. The fortress was
unquestionably monumental and climbing it alone,
much less seizing it from its inhabitants, would have
been no small achievement. If much of the ground
and rock face was covered in patches of snow, the
climb would have been all the more difficult and
dangerous. Alexander called together 300 men who
had shown themselves to be skilled climbers in
previous sieges and set about to reach the fortress'
summit. Upon seeing Alexander's men at the top of
the summit, the fortress commander, Ariamazes,
agreed to unconditional surrender, but Alexander

Facing page: 'Alexander Slaying Cleitus', by Daniel de Blieck (1610–1673). Oil on canvas.

cruelly repaid him for his previous overconfidence, ordering him flogged and crucified. He was much kinder to the daughters of Oxyartes, especially Roxane, with whom, we are told, Alexander fell in love at first sight. Although he lusted mightily after her, he did not force her immediately into his bed, but instead made her his lawful wife, an act that may have raised some eyebrows among his fellow Macedonians, but would have likely served to ameliorate any lingering ill-will that the Sogdian and Bactrian barons may have held toward Alexander, for now one of their own was the wife of their king.

The Murder of Cleitus the Black

Perhaps in the autumn of 328 BCE, Alexander and the Macedonians celebrated a festival in honour of Dionysus, to whom it was the king's custom to make grand sacrifice each year on a specified sacred day. The ceremonies and revels in honour of the wine god soon devolved into a raucous drinking party. Sycophantic admirers among the group heaped flatteries upon the king. They claimed that the achievements of Polydeuces and Castor could not be compared to those of Alexander, feats that had come to rival those of Heracles himself. The mouthy courtiers, although they lavished extravagant praises on Alexander, said nothing of the contributions of the Macedonians who had helped him gain the Persian Empire. Cleitus the Black, the man who

saved Alexander from almost certain death at the Battle of the Granicus, the brother of the king's wet nurse, sat by and listened to the flatterers, objecting not only to the exclusion of any Macedonians beyond Alexander from their praise, but to Alexander's increasing orientalism, his assumption of Persian dress, his full-fledged embrace of Persian court ceremonial and especially the insulting – at least to Macedonians – act of *proskynesis*. For Cleitus, Alexander had ceased to be the first among equals, the typical role of the Macedonian king, a Companion, who led and fought *alongside* his men, not hovering above them like some god.

It is also possible that Cleitus had learned of, or suspected, Alexander's intention to appoint him satrap of Bactria, to replace the aging Artabazus, a move that Cleitus, who had not long before commanded a significant portion of the Companion cavalry, would have viewed as a demotion. The reorganization of the Companions had pushed Cleitus to the fringes. Would he go the way of Philotas, another senior cavalry commander who fell from Alexander's favour? An appointment to the satrapy of Bactria would sentence him, at least in Cleitus' view, to a life of boredom and irrelevance at the edge of the world.

After enduring considerable gushing over Alexander, Cleitus finally spoke. He asserted that Alexander's flatterers had no right to insult the gods by comparing a mortal to them and that he would not allow a compliment to be paid to Alexander 'at the expense of the mighty ones of long ago …' (Arrian, IV.8). Cleitus insisted that such

talk brought not honour to the king, but shame. Cleitus went on to suggest that Philip, too, deserved significant credit for the Macedonians' achievements and perhaps, by comparison, Alexander's accomplishments were quite commonplace. Cleitus, his tongue suitably loosened, raised his hand and cried, 'This is the hand that saved you, Alexander, on that day' (Arrian, IV.8). In a fit of drunken rage, Alexander sprang to his feet, grabbed a spear from one of his attendants, and ran Cleitus through. It is likely that Cleitus merely articulated feelings held by many about their king. Alexander's behaviour had grown increasingly ostentatious. His circle of intimates had grown increasingly smaller, his taste for flattery increasingly difficult to quench.

Almost immediately, Alexander felt grievous regret for his impetuous act of violence. He had killed a long-time friend and a man to whom he literally owed his life. A person of deep religious sensitivities, Alexander may also have very quickly been consumed with the terrifying conviction that he had in some way offended the god of wine and madness, the two elements that most contributed to the night's tragedy. It was Dionysus, whose festival Alexander had celebrated earlier the same evening. And Dionysus' most common response to insult was to inflict his mad passion upon the offender, who, possessed by the god, often killed an intimate. Cleitus certainly qualified as such. Alexander became despondent. He wept bitterly. He retired, inconsolable, to his tent. He did not emerge for three days. At the age of 28, Alexander had nearly gained the world. But what had he lost?

To India, Babylon and Beyond

Before looking further eastward, Alexander would be forced to deal with two more scandals that would test his hold on power and the loyalties of his men and bring to the fore the complications of being both King of Macedon and Great King of Persia.

The first, which apparently led the king to abort the implementation of *proskynesis* as part of his court ceremonial, can be seen in one of two ways. One could argue, as some of Alexander's men, perhaps including Cleitus, did, that since his meeting with the oracle at Siwah, Alexander increasingly embraced and promoted his godlike status. His embrace of a practice of ritual obeisance that

Facing page: 'The Battle between Alexander and Porus' by Dutch painter Nicolaes Pieterzoon Berchem (1620–83).

Right: Fragment of terracotta vase showing Alexander as Helios Kosmokrator ('deified ruler of the universe'), from Amisos (modern Samsun), third century BCE, Koninklijke Musea voor Kunst en Geschiedenis, Brussels.

in Greece was reserved for the gods alone, served as compelling evidence that the king had become convinced of his divinity and no longer deigned to traffic among mere mortals. Before, however, we label Alexander a megalomaniac, ill-advisedly shoving his claim to divinity in the face of his mortal Graeco-Macedonian Companions, let us consider that, all along the way, Alexander had mostly proved himself to be a clever and calculating politician. He was now lord of Asia. As such, he presented himself as the heir to the Great Kings of Persia. And the Great Kings of Persia were due ritual obeisance in the form of *proskynesis*. For his Persian subjects, if Alexander were to reject or discard this

Above: Callisthenes of Olynthus (c. 360–328 BCE), Alexander's court historian.

practice, it would be potentially to show himself unworthy of the Great King's diadem, or perhaps worse, disdainful of Persian custom and practice. Alexander, therefore, was forced to engage in a delicate dance to keep the Graeco-Macedonians in his army and his new Persian subjects satisfied.

Proskynesis and the Fall of Callisthenes

At a dinner party comprised of his Macedonian marshals, high-ranking members of the court and senior Persian officials now incorporated into the Macedonian brain trust, the opposition to *proskynesis* trickled into the open. As the banquet began, the Persian officials, one-by-one, fell face first to the floor and grovelled before Alexander as they would any other Great King. One of them slipped while doing so, which elicited chuckles from Leonnatus, who was standing nearby. Alexander flashed his general a harsh glance, after which Leonnatus kept quiet.

On another occasion, however, the issue finally exploded in a way that the king could not ignore. Alexander presided over a symposium wherein he passed around the table a golden cup. In a traditional Persian setting, each man to drink from the cup would be expected to prostrate himself before the Great King, at which time he would receive from the monarch a kiss, perhaps on the mouth or the cheek. As the cup went around the table, each of Alexander's Persian subjects dutifully performed *proskynesis* and received their kisses. But when the cup came to Callisthenes, the court historian, he failed to observe the ritual act.

Alexander was occupied, for the moment, speaking with Hephaestion and did not notice Callisthenes' insolence, but when Callisthenes demanded his kiss, a member of the Companions, Demetrius, the son of Pythonax, shouted to the king that Callisthenes was not due Alexander's kiss since he had not prostrated himself before the king. As such, Alexander denied Callisthenes' kiss and demanded that he perform *proskynesis*. Callisthenes refused and stormed from the dining hall, saying, 'I depart one kiss the poorer' (Arrian, IV.13).

Arrian reports that the incident reflected badly on *both* Alexander and Callisthenes, being suggestive of Alexander's increasing arrogance and Callisthenes' bad manners. As with many scandalous moments in Alexander's career, too much drink probably played a role as well. Callisthenes, the historian and philosopher, relative and student of Aristotle, would have been deeply imbued in Greek values and tradition and a keen student of Greek mythology. He would have believed that to prostrate one's self before any man was to make one's self that man's slave, his pawn, just as all human beings found themselves fragile servants at the mercy of fickle gods. He also, no doubt, saw the non-Greek world as inferior to the Greek, and the Persians in particular as the barbarian 'other'. Their willingness to enslave themselves to a single man, even a king, was the most damning evidence of this fact. It is telling, however, that despite Callisthenes' public affront to Alexander in the mixed company of Persians and Macedonians, the king apparently did not

Left: Alexander the Great kissing Hephaestion, part of a tapestry from Hampton Court, London, UK.

move to punish the court historian immediately. Perhaps he anticipated and accepted the fact that the trappings of Persian court ceremonial would be difficult for Greeks and Macedonians to swallow. Though it is worth noting that the individual who pointed out Callisthenes' failure to perform the ritual act was not a Persian, but a member of the Companions. Even if Demetrius, son of Pythonax, was merely trying to flatter Alexander, his actions certainly point to the fact that not every Greek or Macedonian found *proskynesis* offensive in and of itself.

Some days after Callisthenes' scene, Alexander led a boar hunt, a practice exceedingly common among Macedonian aristocrats, but one that brought into the open the problematic nature of Alexander's dual Macedonian and Persian kingship. In a Macedonian setting, the hunt bore out, in practical application, the king's role as *primus inter pares*, the first among equals. For Macedonians, the hunt was a competition in which the king was a mere participant. The first man to fell the boar, whether he was king or not, was feted and celebrated by his fellow Macedonian aristocrats and the Macedonian king himself would have been the first to raise a toast to the victor of the day's hunt. In fact, even young pages or attendants to Macedonian nobles were allowed to participate in the hunt and, if one of them made a kill, the young man was allowed to recline at dinner with the high Macedonian

Above: Alexander hunting, by Swiss-born engraver Matthäus Merian (1593–1650), as depicted in German chronicler Johann Ludwig Gottfried's *Historische Chronica*, Frankfurt, 1630.

young man was receiving his punishment, whispers circulated that, in fact, Callisthenes had urged the young page toward the misguided act in an attempt to pay Alexander back for the slight he had received days earlier. In doing so, the court historian sowed the seeds of his own demise. For the humiliated Hermolaus plotted revenge against the king, engaging some of his fellow pages in a conspiracy to murder Alexander. By the time the king learned of the plot, Callisthenes' name had been placed among the would-be assassins and what may have begun as a mere attempt at old-school Macedonian one-upmanship evolved into charges of full-blown treason. Although the conspiring pages never named Callisthenes even under torture, the outspoken historian's connection to them now could not be undone.

The pages and Callisthenes were swiftly condemned, the pages stoned to death by members of the Macedonian army. Callisthenes too suffered a grievous fate, although the manner of his death is disputed. We are told alternately that he was tortured and hanged (the torture including having his nose and ears cut off in the manner in which Persian kings dealt with traitors), torn limb from limb by wild animals or dragged around in fetters by the Macedonian army until he eventually died. The preserved testimony of the royal chamberlain, Chares, supports the story of Callisthenes' imprisonment, in spite of the fact that the historian had become a flabby, lice-ridden blowhard. Chares reports that Alexander intended ultimately to ship Callisthenes back to Greece where he would stand

nobles. In the Persian sphere, the hunt would have played out quite differently. No one would dare to shoot anything before the Great King at the risk of being flogged. Only after the Great King had made a kill could other participants join in.

And so it was, that, on this particular day in late 328 or early 327 BCE, a page by the name of Hermolaus dashed to strike a boar before the king. Alexander, hunting almost certainly in mixed company, ordered Hermolaus flogged. While the

trial in the presence of Aristotle. Whatever the case may be, Callisthenes died a cruel death, and likely for no other reason than his loose tongue and poor judgment.

The Invasion of India

By spring 327 BCE, Alexander, having crushed resistance among Persian hold-outs and Macedonian conspirators, prepared to invade India. He and his army crossed the Hindu Kush by way of the Khyber Pass. He divided the army into two columns. Hephaestion and Perdiccas were given command of an advance force of perhaps 8000 men and sent ahead to the Indus. Their orders were to secure the main road. Alexander took the remainder of the army, including the Royal Squadron, the Silver Shields and the Agrianians, and concentrated on the more difficult task of pacifying the mountain peoples north of the river, in the region of the Bajaur and the Swat. The forces of Hephaestion and Perdiccas faced minimal resistance, except at Peucelaotis (probably Charsadda). The recalcitrant governor of the city, Astes, put up a decent fight, but ultimately lost his life in the 30-day siege that followed, after which Hephaestion and Perdiccas entered and garrisoned the city before resuming their trek along the main road to the Indus Valley.

To the north, Alexander made his way into the Kunar Valley, where villagers (the Aspasians) fled

before him into the perceived safety of mountain hideaways. Alexander attacked their positions, but was not able to secure their surrender. Typical of Alexander's campaigns in the Kunar, he and the natives exchanged periodic unsuccessful raids, but Ptolemy, son of Lagus, who now began to emerge as a talented and decisive commander, finally aided the king in bringing the locals to capitulation. About this time, Alexander reached a city called Nysa. At its outskirts, he was approached by an embassy of local leaders, who duly surrendered the city to him.

In Greek myth, it was to a place bearing precisely this name (Nysa) that Zeus took the young Dionysus to shield him from Hera's ire. For, not uncommonly, Zeus had lain with a mortal, Semele, and conceived the child, provoking the anger of his Olympian wife. When Alexander reached the Indian town of Nysa and was shown the ivy that he had doubtless seen his own mother, a known initiate of the Dionysiac rites, wear, he thought he had found the city in question. The words of Dionysus in Euripides must have been ringing in Alexander's ears. After all, they could have been his own:

'Far behind me lie the golden-rivered lands, Lydia and Phrygia, where my journeying began. Overland I went, across the steppes of Persia where the sun strikes hotly down, through Bactrian fastness and

Left: Alexander's army crosses into northeastern Persia, as depicted in this magazine illustration.

Facing page: 'Bacchus Procession' by Flemish baroque painter, Frans Francken II (1581–1642). Oil on wood. State Art Museum, Tula.

the grim wastes of Media. Thence, to rich Arabia
I came, and so all along Asia's swarming littoral of
towered cities where Greeks and foreign nations
mingling live, my progress made. There I taught my
dances to the feet of living men and established my
rites, so that I might be revealed on earth for what I
am: a god.' (Euripides, *Bacchae*, 11–19).

Arrian's account of Alexander's sojourn in Nysa
is also revealing: 'He [Alexander] felt, moreover, that
his Macedonian soldiers would consent to share his
hardships a little longer, if they knew they were in
competition with Dionysus' (V.2). Arrian and Curtius
both suggest that Alexander's men were indeed
inspired by the sight of the ivy and the rumoured
connection of the place to Dionysus. In Arrian, the
men are taken up in 'true Bacchic frenzy' at the foot
of nearby Mt. Merus – *meros* being the Greek word
for 'thigh' and an obvious allusion to the god's second
birth from Zeus. Curtius reports that, although the
soldiers' Bacchic reverie might have been feigned,
Alexander and his army engaged thereafter in a
10-day festival in Dionysus' honour (VIII.10.17–18).
By these festivities, Alexander may have hoped
that, if Dionysus' anger had somehow contributed
to Cleitus' death, the king could here return to
the god's good graces. After the recent tensions at
court, with the murder of Cleitus, the Philotas affair,
proskynesis, Callisthenes and the pages' plot, a little
extra motivation and celebration for Alexander's men
would have been a welcome respite indeed.

**Right: The Rock of Aornos (modern Pir-Sar), which bested
Heracles but not Alexander.**

The Aornos Rock

It is likely after the revels at Nysa that Alexander rendezvoused with Hephaestion and Perdiccas before hearing of further resistance in the Swat Valley to the north. When Alexander entered the Swat, he was met by Craterus, who had been left to monitor the region, and from whom he learned that the rebels had retreated to the fortress of the Aornos Rock (modern Pir-Sar), another place with profound connections to Greek legend, for the mighty Rock, with its precipitous and sheer wall, had baffled even the great Heracles, who tried to scale it and failed. The chance to surpass Heracles was too tempting to pass up. Arrian writes that Alexander was seized with 'a passionate desire to capture it (the Rock) and the story about Heracles was not the least of his incentives' (IV.28). Although some historians have viewed Alexander's assault on the Aornos Rock as a meaningless diversion, it is worth remembering that it was defended by the leaders of several recalcitrant tribes from the Bajaur and Swat Valleys. Taking it would, no doubt, have had strategic significance as well, at least as Alexander might have seen it, namely the collapse of further resistance north of the Indus. Who would dare challenge the man who conquered the Rock that bested even Heracles?

Pir-Sar lay just west of the Indus on one side and was surrounded by a sheer ravine on the others, making it difficult for Alexander to employ his siege works. Alexander ordered that nearby trees be felled to bridge the gully and to serve as the foundation for an earthen mound that would allow

him to move at least some siege engines into place. The engines would launch cover fire for a climbing party that would attempt to commandeer the Rock. Alexander's first crack at scaling Aornos failed. He led an advance guard up the cliff face, for he himself wanted to be first over the 2133m (7000ft) high rock wall, but, when they had nearly reached the top, Alexander sent some of his men ahead to scout the position of the Rock's defenders. The men were immediately crushed by boulders thrown over the rock wall and Alexander and the climbing party had to beat a hasty retreat to the bottom. In celebration of having successfully thwarted Alexander's attack, the defenders danced and beat drums through the night, the sounds of which undoubtedly irked the frustrated Alexander.

The king spent the next two days reconsidering his assault on the rock, or perhaps reformulating his plan. Shifting the positions of his siege engines slightly, he was ready to try again, this time leading the Silver Shields up the Rock. The Silver Shields' agility and ability to deflect oncoming missiles, thought Alexander, made them ideal candidates for the task at hand. This second attempt achieved its object and Alexander even succeeded in his desire to be first over the wall, although he did sustain a fairly significant wound. The taking of the Aornos Rock was, in some respects, as great a feat as the siege of Tyre, the culmination of a series of innovations and masterstrokes in the art of siege

Facing page: The army of Alexander, crossing the river Indus, fights at the Battle of Hydaspes (from a fifteenth century French manuscript, 'Life of Alexander').

warfare under Philip and Alexander. Alexander himself had proven a brilliant besieger, digesting and learning from what setbacks he incurred and devising often ingenious strategies to overcome these obstacles.

With resistance in the Swat Valley definitively subdued, Alexander crossed the Indus via a pontoon bridge constructed by Hephaestion during the siege of Aornos, after which he came to the city of Taxila, where he was welcomed with gifts by the Indian prince, Taxiles, ruler of the realm between the Indus and the Hydaspes (Jhelum) River to the east. The Punjab now lay open to Alexander, a land beyond the reaches of the former Great King's empire. As Alexander allowed his men a month of rest, he must have considered what he might find there. Perhaps he was soon to reach the Outer Sea, the edge of the world. One thing is certain: Alexander's insatiable curiosity drove him to find out.

The Battle of the Hydaspes

The last and perhaps greatest battle of Alexander's career took place in late Spring 326 BCE. It pitted Alexander against the Indian king of Parauva, Porus, whose domain stretched east from the Hydaspes River in the Punjab to the Acesines (Chenab) River. If Alexander's march into India was to continue, he would be forced to reckon with Porus, a task made more difficult by the fact that the Hydaspes was at

full swell in the midst of India's monsoon season. Alexander first determined to cross the river near Haranpur, about 177km (110 miles) from Taxila. With the monsoon rains setting in and the already turbulent river now threatening to overspill its banks, the crossing would not be easy.

In addition, Porus, who had been making preparations for Alexander's arrival since the king was welcomed at Taxila in the territory of his enemy, Taxiles, had stationed his army on the opposite bank, including a large number of Indian war elephants. Looking across at the mighty beasts, Alexander considered how his cavalry horses would respond. The Macedonians had seen war elephants once before, the minor contingent of 15 that served Darius at Gaugamela (as opposed to some 200 presently under Porus' command), but they apparently had not played a significant role in that battle and, certainly, they had not occupied the front lines of the enemy formation as Porus' elephants did here. Alexander knew well that the combination of the rising river and the elephants created a major obstacle to his crossing. Initially, he declared his intention to wait until the waters fell.

But when the river failed to cooperate, Alexander instead engaged a tactical ruse whereby

Right: An Indian war elephant, with a howdah, a platform or carriage placed atop the animal's back, from which missiles (javelins or arrows) could be fired.

Diversion at the Hydaspes

'Between the island and the main camp of which Craterus was left in charge, Meleager, Attalus and Gorgias were posted with the mercenary cavalry and infantry; their instructions, too, were to effect a crossing in sections as soon as they saw that the Indians were fairly engaged. The mounted troops which Alexander selected to operate under his own command consisted of the special squadron of the Companions, the cavalry regiments of Hephaestion, Perdiccas and Demetrius, the contingents from Bactria and Sogdiana, the Scythian cavalry and the mounted archers from Daae; from the infantry units he chose the Guards, the battalions of Cleitus (the White) and Coenus, the archers and the Agrianes.

He took the precaution of moving at some distance from the river, in order to conceal his march to the point where he would cross – the island, namely, and the spit of land opposite to it. To this point the floats had already been conveyed some time previously, and now, under cover of darkness, they were filled with hay and carefully sewn up. During the night a deluge of rain helped to conceal the preparations for the coming attempt; the clatter of arms, shouted orders, and the commotion they caused could not be heard across the river through the noise of the storm and the claps of thunder.'

ARRIAN, V.13

he would bring his men to the banks of the river each night and order the blaring of trumpets and the war cry to be raised, leading Porus to prepare for battle. But the battle would not be joined and Alexander's men would simply withdraw to camp. For several nights running, Alexander performed the same ploy, but at a spot slightly farther upstream each time. Alexander had received intelligence about the location of a small, densely-wooded spit of land, not far from an uninhabited island that lay in the middle of the river in a bend upstream. It was there that he decided to cross. He hoped that the combination of the foliage and the island would provide enough cover that his crossing would be as easy and inconspicuous as possible. But, in a bold and risky stratagem, he would leave Craterus and a majority of the army on the eastern banks near Haranpur in hopes that Porus too would fix the bulk of his forces there. Alexander's upstream feints had served as both scouting mission and diversion. He knew the lay of the land that ran between Haranpur and the tiny strip where he would attempt to cross and he had prevented Porus from suspecting his intentions because each night he would return to his original position without having attempted the crossing.

The river that Alexander now needed to cross was far more formidable than the Granicus – wide, torrid and bursting its banks. The crossing would require a flotilla and galleys to transport the men and horses. In the days prior to the crossing, Alexander had sneaked materials with which he would build his rafts to the site of the crossing, in hopes that the construction activities would be obscured by the foliage in the river's bend. His preparations were completed the night before the battle in a torrential downpour that further masked his activities.

Ready for the crossing, Alexander, accompanied by Hephaestion, Ptolemy, Perdiccas and Seleucus, plunged into the river, with Craterus holding his position at the original site. The forces they led were mostly cavalry, although contingents of infantry, the Silver Shields, Agrianians and archers joined them as well. Some of the archers were given mounts, a seemingly new tactic in Alexander's strategic arsenal; perhaps they were meant to fire

Left: At the Hydaspes, Porus musters his war elephants in preparation for battle with Alexander.

into and disorient and immobilize Porus' elephants or to knock their drivers from their backs. The majority of the infantry held firm with Craterus, awaiting the success of Alexander's crossing. The rains, the woods, the island and Alexander's repeated feints had indeed afforded him the element of surprise.

By the time Porus realized that the Macedonian king was crossing the river, Alexander was almost to the other side. Before Porus' cavalry and chariots, under the command of his son, had time to make any successful foray to Alexander's position, he had been able to marshal his troops. Porus' detachment of forces to Alexander's position was Craterus' signal to begin his own crossing. Porus' son probably commanded about 2000 horsemen and a significant number of chariots. When he heard that Porus' forces were moving against him, Alexander seems to have first dispatched his mounted archers, perhaps thinking that Porus had sent his main army with its vast contingent of elephants. But when he learned that only Porus' cavalry approached his position, he took his place at the head of the Royal Squadron and ordered staggered cavalry charges. Initial skirmishing left 400 Indians dead, including the commander of the detachment, Porus' son. The remaining horses and chariots turned to flee, the large Indian chariots stuck in the thick, rain-soaked mud and were quickly abandoned. In this early fighting, Bucephalus received a significant wound,

Facing page: Copper engraving of duel between Alexander the Great and King Porus of Paurava, manuscript of 'Romance of Alexander', Russia, c. 1840.

Right: Alexander and his army battle Porus and his war elephants at the Hydaspes.

but the tireless old war horse fought on at his master's bidding.

The Phalanx versus Elephants

When Porus learned of the failure of his cavalry detachment, he faced a difficult choice. Send the main force of his army against Alexander, or hold his position in hopes of preventing Craterus' passage across the river. He decided on the former, leaving only a small force of troops and elephants to deny Craterus the riverbank. As Porus advanced toward Alexander through deep soft mud, he sought a spot where abundant river sand made the ground harder and allowed more manoeuvrability, especially critical to his chariot forces. Porus found ground solid enough to draw up his infantry and he did so on an extended front, his centre occupied by infantry with an elephant positioned every 30m (100ft) or so.

To give them time to recover, Alexander used his cavalry forces as a kind of screen, riding up and down the enemy lines until his infantry phalanx was ready to join battle. Alexander was careful not to engage the Indian centre just yet. He needed his phalanx to deal with Porus' elephants, because he still feared the possibility that his horses would be reticent to attack the elephants directly. The heavy

infantry with their massive *sarissas* would have
taken more time to muster than Alexander's speedy
cavalry regiments. This, combined with the fatigue
that the heavy infantry felt, having endured an
arduous river crossing and a not insignificant march
through dense river mud to meet Porus, would
have meant they needed some time to recover and
prepare to fall into formation.

When Alexander's infantry battalions were
ready to join the fight, they took their positions and
Alexander rode to take his place on the Macedonian
right. Coenus commanded the cavalry forces on
the left. The two led a coordinated attack whereby
Alexander deployed his mounted archers against
the enemy's left flank, causing enough confusion
and disarray that the Indians had to pull forces from
the right to supplement the ranks on the left. With
the Indian troops from the right moving to relieve
Porus' left flank, Alexander and Coenus launched
near-simultaneous cavalry charges, and Porus'
unfortunate army found itself under attack from
both directions. At this point the Indian flanks,
being driven back by the Macedonian cavalry on
both sides, retreated into the Indian centre.

In the infantry fighting, Porus' elephants did
their worst and some, in fact, to use Arrian's phrase,
'dealt destruction' in the Macedonian phalanx,
trampling infantrymen underfoot and impaling
others with their huge tusks. But, as they had
against the Persian scythed chariots at Gaugamela,
the Macedonian infantry eluded the greatest part
of the elephant corps by opening their ranks and
allowing the massive beasts to run through the lines.

But instead of allowing them to pass all the way through, the phalangites stood at either side of the great beasts, using their long *sarissas* to dislodge the elephant drivers from the elephants' backs and thereafter to drive the animals back into their own lines. The now driverless and uncontrollable elephants began to trample the front lines of the Indian forces sending them into complete disarray, while the disciplined Macedonian phalanx returned to formation.

At this point, the remainder of Porus' forces made up one body that was effectively surrounded by Alexander's forces on three sides. Porus' cavalry was able to make one last gasp charge, directed straight at Alexander's position in hopes of killing the king and turning the tide of the battle, but Alexander's superior cavalry successfully repelled the charge, annihilating almost the entire remainder of the Indian cavalry in the process. Porus' forces now began to flee, but the brave rajah himself remained in his howdah, upon the largest of the Indian war elephants, and held his ground even as the great majority of his army fled in terror. He fought on, hurling javelins at the Macedonians and, only when he himself was severely wounded, losing blood and perhaps on the verge of losing consciousness, did the ferocious Porus retreat. Alexander sent a small group led by his Indian ally Taxiles to retrieve Porus. Even as Taxiles rode upon the weary Porus' elephant, the king turned his beast and prepared to

Facing page: The Macedonian phalanx prepares for an elephant attack at the Battle of Hydaspes.

fight once more. At this point, Porus' wound likely got the better of him and he simply could no longer carry on. Craterus, who had, by this time, crossed the Hydaspes with his troops and who seemed to have played no role in the battle whatsoever, at least if we are to believe our sources, tracked down and slaughtered the remnants of Porus' fleeing army. Craterus' trooped were also likely tasked with

Above: A scene from 'Alexander the Great and Porus', by Charles Le Brun (1665). Louvre, Paris.

Alexander and Porus

'Alexander, informed of his approach, rode out to meet him, accompanied by a small part of his Companions. When they met, he reined in his horse, and looked at his adversary in admiration: he was a magnificent figure of a man, over seven feet high and one of great personal beauty; his bearing had lost none of its pride; his air was one of a brave man meeting another, of a king in the presence of a king, with whom he had fought honourably for his kingdom.'

ARRIAN, V.19

Right: Silver tetradrachm of Alexander, minted c. 324 BCE, depicting Alexander astride Bucephalus attacking Porus (on a war elephant) at the Hydaspes. The coin, perhaps minted at Babylon, may be the only depiction of Alexander from his own lifetime to have survived.

corralling the surviving elephants, which Alexander would now incorporate into his army.

When, after the battle, Porus was at last brought before Alexander, a man who Arrian and Diodorus agree was over 2m (7ft) tall (the point being he was a large man in comparison to the smallish Greeks and Macedonians), the Macedonian king, impressed with his opponent's indomitable fighting spirit, asked the rajah how he would like to be treated. Porus' response, probably given through an interpreter, was simply, 'as a king would' (Arrian, V.19). Alexander responded by allowing Porus to remain the sovereign of his territories, acting as a kind of client king. Porus, perhaps as impressed with Alexander as Alexander was with him, and moved by the king's gracious gesture, remained loyal to his new Macedonian overlord for the remainder of his life.

Eulogy of the Hydaspes and Bucephalus

Through masterful strategy and sheer force of will, Alexander had achieved definitive victory. And, even given some of our ancient sources propensity for exaggeration, it is clear that he did so with less than half of his total forces and perhaps considerably fewer than half. We never hear of Craterus and his troops joining the fight, although one has to take into account the fact that the sources are always more concerned with what *Alexander* is doing. Their accounts of his battles focus their greatest attentions on the king's movements during the fighting. The extant descriptions of the Hydaspes are no exception.

Nevertheless, the historian might rightly conclude, all things considered, that this muddy, bloody engagement on the banks of a river nearly 6437km (4000 miles), as the crow flies, from Pella, was Alexander's greatest moment as military strategist and battlefield general.

In that moment of triumph, however, he lost his greatest battlefield asset, and most loyal friend. For almost two decades, Alexander had ridden his great black steed, Bucephalus. He had been astride his mighty war horse when he at last brought the Persian Empire to its knees. Arrian says that no one ever rode Bucephalus except Alexander, because the horse would allow none but the king to mount him (V.19). Alexander had even taught the horse to kneel in full battle regalia, so that he might mount him from the ground. Wounded in the initial skirmish with Porus' son at the riverbank, the mighty horse did not yield and he did not succumb to his injuries until the battle was won.

We would expect nothing less from the greatest of all war horses. Some authorities, convinced of Bucephalus' invincibility, claimed that he had, in fact, not died of his wounds, but rather, of old age. And, in their defence, it is likely that Bucephalus would have been at least approaching his middle twenties in 326 BCE (Arrian says he was about 30). Just as Philip had wished when he saw his young son break the prized stallion, Bucephalus

Left: Images of Alexander and Bucephalus; training of Bucephalus by Alexander, pursuit of Darius, and Alexander and Bucephalus on a lion hunt. Fifteenth-century Greek manuscript, Bibliotheque Nationale, Paris.

Bucephalus: The Greatest of All War Horses

'Near the scene of the battle and the spot where he crossed the Hydaspes, Alexander founded two cities; one he called Nicaea to commemorate his victory, the other Bucephala, in memory of his horse Bucephalus, who died in that country – not of hurts received in battle, but of old age and exhaustion. He was about thirty and worn out. In former days he had shared with Alexander many a danger and many a weary march. No one ever rode him but his master, for he would never permit anyone else to mount him. He was a big horse, high-spirited – a noble creature; he was branded with the figure of an ox-head, whence his name – though some have said that the name came from a white mark on his head, shaped like the head of an ox. This was the only bit of white on his body, all the rest of him being black. In Uxia, once, Alexander lost him, and issued an edict that he would kill every man in the country unless he was brought back – as he promptly was. The story is evidence both of the fear which Alexander inspired and of his devotion to Bucephalus. But I must say no more: what I have written in Bucephalus' praise, I have written for Alexander's sake.'

ARRIAN, V.20

had carried Alexander to a kingdom that was (almost) large enough for his imagination. It is fitting that Bucephalus' last battle would prove to be Alexander's last full-scale engagement, as well. On the banks of the very river where Bucephalus made his last crossing, Alexander founded a city and named it Bucephala. He also held a funeral procession for his fallen companion, which he led himself, and set up a grand grave monument in the horse's honour. The horse became so legendary, so closely associated with the exploits and the 'myth' of Alexander, that the Successors (the *Diadochoi*) portrayed him on their coinage, sometimes even bearing the horns of Zeus-Ammon. Like his master, Bucephalus would become divine, a visceral and immediate symbol of power. One of our sources, Arrian, even provides him with an eloquent eulogy, which ends with a profound disclaimer, 'what I have written in Bucephalus' praise,' he writes, 'I have written for Alexander's sake' (V.20).

The End of Alexander's World

As one might expect, Alexander was not content with Porus' kingdom and he pressed on toward the Acesines River. By the time Alexander encamped on its banks, the monsoon rains were pelting his army at their fiercest rate yet and the nearby river was flooding its banks. Alexander and his men made the crossing nonetheless, a truly dangerous gamble, even without enemies occupying the opposite bank. East of the river, they faced periodic resistance, most notably from the tribesmen near the city of Sangala (in the vicinity of Lahore and Amritsar, although not definitively identified). When the Indians retreated to the citadel of Sangala, Alexander's Macedonians again proved themselves masters of siege warfare. Although they

Below: Alexander the Great builds a city as a memorial to Bucephalus, from a c.1420 French copy of *Historia de Proeliis* (vellum). British Library, London.

suffered a significant number of wounded, Arrian puts that number at 1200 (V.24), the Macedonians would ultimately bring the Indian hold-outs to submission.

As the driving rains continued to fall, Porus showed up to help with fresh troops and additional elephants. The walls were breached and the city stormed. Alexander allowed his men to sack and plunder the city, perhaps sensing their growing frustration, at least at the appalling weather conditions, if not the fact that they were still campaigning with no apparent end in sight. When the city had been sacked to Alexander's satisfaction, he handed it over to Porus and allowed him to install his own garrison force there. Alexander now proceeded to the Hyphasis (Beas) River, facing no further opposition along the way. As the army encamped near the riverbank, rumours began to swirl about the new dangers that lay beyond another swollen river: fiercer, more warlike peoples than they had encountered to date and monsters even more terrible than Porus' war elephants.

There were murmurs in camp as well about the campaign's goal, its ultimate end and whether Alexander even imagined such a thing or if, for Alexander, there was only the end of the world, wherever, whenever and however dangerous that might be to find. Diodorus adds that the monsoon rains had lasted 70 days, a fact that had, no doubt, significantly dampened the morale of the troops

Left: 'The Onward Sweep of Mighty Alexander', by Dudley Tennant (1867–1952).

(XII.94.3). When the whispers of discontent grew to a low roar and Alexander could no longer ignore his men's frustrations, he called the army together and gave a speech. In it, he evoked the exploits of Heracles and Dionysus and affirmed that he and his army had surpassed them. And he also declared enthusiastically that 'to this empire there will be no boundaries, but what the God himself has made for the whole world' (Arrian, V.26).

This statement, for Alexander, represented a passionate conviction. It was a passion that had not ebbed and, perhaps, his men feared, would not. It was exactly the type of thing that they did not want to hear. It served as evidence, straight from the mouth of their king, that their campaign not only had no clear end at that moment; it might, in fact, never have one. And so, when Alexander's speech was ended, a hushed silence fell over the army until, at last, Coenus, son of Polemocrates, one of Alexander's most senior generals, a man of unassailable character and reputation, gathered his courage, stepped forward and spoke. His respectful and pragmatic speech to his king ended with the following words: 'Sir, if there is one thing above all others a successful man should know, it is when to stop. Assuredly for a commander like yourself, with an army like ours, there is nothing to fear from any enemy; but fortune remember is an unpredictable thing, and against what it may bring no man has any defence' (Arrian V.28). Coenus' speech was met with applause and not a few tears. Alexander's exhausted army had made its decision and the king, like his ancestor Achilles before him, retired angrily to his quarters. The next morning, with anger turned to resolve, Alexander called a meeting of his generals and informed them that he would not force a single Macedonian to accompany him further, but he himself would go on, regardless. But the collected commanders called Alexander's bluff and still refused. The sulking Alexander withdrew again to spend the next two days brooding alone in his tent. Alexander may have hoped in those hours alone that his men would change their minds, that his tantrum or their fear of repercussion may, after some point, make an impression. But, eventually, he would have realized that the longer he isolated himself, the more ultimately humiliating the acceptance of his army's decision would be. And Alexander knew one thing for certain: all that he had accomplished across 18,105km (11,250 miles) and eight years of marches, he had not done alone. In the end, Cleitus was right. Alexander had been accompanied by the greatest army the world had ever seen, an army assembled by his father Philip, even if perfected by himself, and his commanders from top to bottom, dead or alive, had proved themselves worthy to be called his Companions, if not his equals. Now, he must honour them.

At the end of the second day, Alexander emerged from his tent and declared that he would leave the decision to the gods. He would make sacrifice before the river and read the omens. If those omens proved unfavourable, he would accept the will of his men and turn back. This, of course, was a face-saving manoeuver. Alexander was beaten. He was not bowed. He would not suffer to endure public

Above: Alexander observes the Hydaspes River, with Porus' war elephants in the background.

Right: Alexander arrives at a temple in India. From a Persian manuscript, British Museum, London.

humiliation. He would not shame himself before the men he had led across the world. And so he called for sacrificial victims and the gods put an end to Alexander's amazing journey on the banks of the Hyphasis River.

Arrian records that shouts of jubilation rose up through the ranks when the news was announced; grizzled veterans wept and embraced, and man after man came to Alexander's tent afterward praising him, thanking him and calling down the gods' blessings upon him for allowing them to prevail. It was, Arrian goes on, 'the only defeat he had ever suffered' (V.29).

Toward the Outer Ocean

By September 326 BCE, Alexander's army had again reached the sight of their great victory at the Battle of the Hydaspes, to the settlements of Nicaea and Bucephala, which had been heavily damaged by the ravaging monsoon rains. In his absence, Alexander had ordered his engineers to begin a massive ship-building initiative, as he had envisioned, at some point, sailing down the river, which he hoped emptied into the Outer Sea. If his eastern march would not take him there, perhaps the waters of the Hydaspes and Indus would.

The cost of building the flotilla of warships, troop and horse galleys and supply barges that may have totalled as many as 2000 vessels would have been significant, as would the commitment of labour to complete the operation. Monsoon season would have crippled Alexander's supply lines to some degree and he may have been short on portable monies. Harpalus, the king's treasurer-general, still had access to considerable resources. Commandeering the fortune of the Great King of Persia had made Alexander an extremely wealthy man. Getting those monies to Alexander's location in a timely fashion was another matter altogether.

Still, Alexander made do, but his plight was complicated by factors that he could not control. One was the passing of Coenus, one of the ablest of all his generals. In addition, the increasing rivalry between Hephaestion and Craterus was becoming thorny indeed. The two men had a very public argument that devolved into blows in the wake of the Battle of the Hydaspes, probably because Hephaestion had chastised Craterus for not crossing the river or joining the fighting with sufficient speed. The dispute was now spreading through the ranks of their individual troops and hindering their ability to work together.

The tensions became so great that, when the river fleet was ready to launch and Alexander organized contingents of men to march ahead along the riverbank to reconnoitre, meet potential resistance and defend the fleet, if necessary, Craterus and his men were instructed to march along the right bank of the river, and Hephaestion and his along the left.

Boarding his ship, Alexander poured libations into the water from a golden bowl, invoking the god of the river and asking it, Heracles, Ammon and Poseidon for safe passage. The Royal Squadron, the Silver Shields, the archers and the Agrianians embarked on transport ships under Alexander's personal command with Nearchus appointed admiral of the fleet.

The Campaign against the Mallians and a Near-Fatal Wound

On the third day of the voyage, Alexander received word that the Mallians and the Oxydracae, two formidable warlike tribes in the lower Punjab, had agreed to join forces and prevent the Macedonians from travelling through their territory. Alexander sought to meet these peoples individually before they could join forces. In roughly two days, he had reached the territory of the Mallians, where he disembarked and began operations to pacify the region. The final result was the siege of another hilltop fortress, another bloody and dangerous adventure that ultimately found Alexander the first man over the enemy battlements, wounded by an arrow in the chest, surrounded by Mallian warriors, and fighting for his life. The Mallians were apparently very skilled at cutting or throwing down scaling ladders and they did so with such haste that Alexander's men could barely get over the wall to rescue him. When they did and turned the fight in the Macedonians' direction, one man after another was forced to hold his shield over Alexander's prone body as he writhed in pain from his wound.

At last, the Macedonians gained the upper hand and an all-out slaughter ensued. Men, women and children fell by raging Macedonian swords. When the fighting ended, Alexander demanded that Perdiccas cut the arrow from his chest, as no doctor was at hand. Perdiccas obliged. As he pulled the barb from Alexander's body, blood rushed from the wound and the king fainted, some believing he was dead. For several days he could not be moved. There was serious concern among his intimates that he would not survive and rumours circulated among the greater part of his army that the king had, in fact, died. Although, as usual, Alexander defied the odds, his fighting days had come to an end.

When Alexander was well enough to be moved, albeit by means of a litter, he had himself carried to the river and shipped downstream to the Macedonian camp at the junction of the Hydraotes and the Acesines. When the troops first caught sight of the recumbent Alexander, they thought they were only seeing his corpse, but, at last, the vessel made its way to the river bank and the still-ailing but defiant Alexander raised his hand and greeted his men. The men in the camp raised shouts of joy. When a party of guards arrived with a stretcher to transport Alexander to his tent, he refused and instead called for his horse. At the sight of Alexander astride a horse once again, there was, according to Arrian, 'a storm of applause so loud that the riverbanks and neighbouring glens re-echoed with noise' (VI.13). As he rode to his tent, the men blessed him and showered him with wreaths and garlands.

As Alexander recovered, the collected wisdom of the army, and probably at this point Alexander himself, was that a return to Persia and perhaps to Babylon would now be in the best interest of all. Alexander's plan seems to have been to sail down

Facing page: Alexander, wounded, passes through his fleet on the Hydraotis to reassure his men that he is recovering and to quell rumours of his demise. His men rejoice and cheer, throwing garlands of flowers as he passes.

the Indus river, with the support of a land army on the banks as before, to the Outer Sea (Arabian Sea/Indian Ocean), then sail northwest to the Persian Gulf and along the Babylonian coast and up the Euphrates River to Babylon. The voyage would not be without its potential dangers and the army would not be able to shadow the fleet the entire way, but the voyage's success would open up a safe, fast route from the Persian heartland to India, something that would be a great boon to Alexander and the future administration of his empire. But the voyage did not go as planned. India's monsoon winds made the river unnavigable in places and delayed the fleet. The impatient Alexander decided to lead the land army ahead to prepare the way for the fleet when weather conditions would allow the voyage to continue. He first sent Craterus and much of the heavy infantry ahead toward Carmania (about halfway back to Babylon) through an inland road via the Mulla Pass. Alexander struck out with a force of perhaps 40,000 men, leaving the fleet behind him. At first, he found the territory hospitable enough and was able to replenish his stores of fresh water from wells dug in the desert around Patala.

Alexander even founded a new city shortly thereafter, sometime in the autumn of 325 BCE, Rhambacia (Bela), 200km (124 miles) west of Karachi and there he left Leonnatus with a

contingent of troops with orders to keep the locals pacified and prepare for the arrival of Nearchus and the fleet. Alexander pressed west into Gedrosia with the understanding that, as long as he remained near the coast, he would be able to replenish his water supply by digging wells. But when he reached the mountains of the Talar-i-Bund along the Makran coast, which stretched all the way to the sea, he was forced to make a significant inland detour. It would have disastrous consequences.

The Gedrosian Desert

Alexander and his troops now entered a barren, hellish wasteland. Soaring temperatures in the inhospitable desert forced Alexander to march mostly at night, sometimes 121km (75 miles) to find brackish wells with barely drinkable water. When suitable water was found after a long, dry march, some men drank so immoderately that they sickened, or even, if we are to believe Arrian, killed themselves (VI.26). Animals began to die *en masse*. The thick, sinking sand would have been extremely hard on horses and pack animals and the heat and lack of water would have sealed their fate. Some hardy animals that did survive were killed by ravenous men as rations ran dangerously low. If Alexander's initial detour upon reaching the coastal mountains is understandable, the continuance of his journey into hostile desert is more difficult to reconcile. We are told, however, that Alexander had heard stories that the legendary Assyrian queen, Semiramis, and Cyrus the Great, the founder of the Achaemenid Empire, had attempted and failed to

Above: Alexander the Great's army crossing the inhospitable coastal desert of Baluchistan, Makran (the Gedrosian desert), while vultures swarm over head.

cross the Gedrosian desert. Alexander's insistence to press on under the appalling conditions he encountered in Gedrosia may well represent his hubristic attempt to outstrip two of his most renowned Near Eastern predecessors.

Other stories circulated among the ancients that the march through Gedrosia was somehow Alexander's way of punishing his men for their mutiny at the Hyphasis, but surely if this were the case Alexander would not have subjected himself to such harsh torments. And what of the men with Nearchus and Craterus, or those he left with Leonnatus at Rhambacia? Where they too not deserving of punishment? The plain fact of the matter is that Alexander had devised a sound plan to support, defend and provision the fleet as it made its way back to Babylon. When weather conditions temporarily prevented the fleet from travelling the river, Alexander made the quite logical choice to march ahead.

And even when he reached the Gedrosian no man's land, he may have anticipated that going forward would have been quicker and more prudent than turning back toward the coast. The king ably endured the same hardships as his men. He comforted and encouraged them and, in Arrian's famous story, he even refused to drink water unless they enjoyed the same luxury. But 60 days in a terrible, sun-baked wasteland and many lives lost (although, perhaps, not as many as our sources

Facing page: In this modern illustration, Alexander refuses water in the Gedrosian Desert.

relate) would take its toll. Alexander could not get back to Babylon soon enough.

Alexander, at last, reached Pura in the Bampur Basin, where foodstuffs awaited his famished men. Alexander had sent desperate messages as he reached the desert's edge to Stasanor, satrap of Dragania, who sent supplies on the backs of racing camels that arrived at the meagerly-provisioned Gedrosian capital about the same time as Alexander's arrival. After allowing his men a few days' rest, during which they ate and drank their fill, Alexander marched on toward Carmania, through the valley of the Halil Rud. As Alexander crossed the Carmanian border, he met Craterus and his troops along the road, along with convoys bursting with food and livestock. When they reached the city (of Carmania), we are told that seven days of Dionysian revels and excesses ensued. The horrors of the Gedrosian desert would not easily be forgotten, but a week-long orgy of feasting and drunken debauchery could at least act as salve on still-open wounds.

The Mass Marriages at Susa

In the following summer of 324 BCE, Alexander held a grand celebration at Susa. Its purpose: to unite symbolically and in practical application the Macedonian and Persian hierarchies and to cement the foundations of Alexander's new world empire. In a mass wedding ceremony, he gave the daughters of high-ranking Persian nobles to his marshals. For himself, he took the hand of Darius' eldest daughter, Stateira (sometimes called Barsine). He was, of

Alexander's Noblest Deed?

'The army was crossing a desert of sand; the sun was already blazing down upon them. But they were struggling on under the necessity of reaching water, which was still far away. Alexander, like everyone else, was tormented by thirst, but he was none the less marching on foot at the head of his men. It was all he could do to keep going, but he did so, and the result (as always) was that the men were better able to endure their misery when they saw that it was equally shared. As they toiled on, a party of light infantry which had gone off looking for water found some – just a wretched little trickle collected in a shallow gully. They scooped up with difficulty what they could and hurried back, with their priceless treasure, to Alexander; then, just before they reached him, they tipped the water into a helmet and gave it to him. Alexander, with a word of thanks for the gift, took the helmet and, in full view of his troops, poured the water on the ground. So extraordinary was the effect of this action that the water wasted by Alexander was as good as a drink for every man in the army. I cannot praise this act too highly; it was a proof, if anything was, not only of his power of endurance, but also of his genius for leadership.'

ARRIAN, VI.26.

172

Above: Wedding of Alexander and Stateira II (Barsine), daughter of Darius III, at Susa.

Facing page: Alexander and his lieutenants celebrate the mass marriages at Susa.

course, already married to Roxane, but polygamy was an accepted social practice among Macedonian kings, despite his mother Olympias' protestations to the contrary. By means of his two wives (and perhaps a third according to Aristobulus' account) Alexander linked himself with the former Persian royal house (of Darius III) and prominent Bactrian nobility

(by Roxane and her father Oxyartes of Bactria). He wedded Hephaestion to Drypetis, another of Darius' daughter's and to Craterus he gave Amastrines, the daughter of Darius' brother. Perdiccas was given a daughter of Atropates, governor of Media. And Ptolemy was given Artacama, the daughter of Artabazus. Seleucus was wed to the daughter of Alexander's troublesome opponent, the now dead warlord Spitamenes. Nearchus, Eumenes, and 70 or 80 more Macedonian nobles received Persian and Iranian wives as well. Alexander himself graciously paid the dowry for each of the days bridegrooms. He also lavished gifts upon all Greeks and Macedonians who had previously wed Persian wives, the number of whom was said to have exceeded 10,000.

It was a grandiose and dramatic gesture, carried out in typical Persian fashion, with requisite Persian excess. And it was vintage Alexander. The purpose of the ceremony would seem straightforward enough. The empire of Alexander could not succeed by being Greek or Macedonian or Persian alone, and it certainly could not succeed if tensions lingered or erupted between Macedonians and Persians. Alexander, perhaps, *at last* had grown weary of fighting, of dissension, of rebellion, of long marches and bloody sieges. In the summer of 324 BCE, he sought, in the most public manner he could imagine, to bring together, once and for all, the variegated peoples of his far-flung empire, the largest empire that had ever been attained.

Above: **Bronze head of Hephaestion (d. 324 BCE), from the Prado Museum, Madrid.**

Right: **Early third-century BCE lion hunt mosaic (pebble mosaic), depicting Alexander and perhaps Hephaestion or Craterus, from the Macedonian royal palace at Pella.**

The Death of Hephaestion

Within three months of the wedding ceremonies, Alexander's beloved Hephaestion was dead. He had developed a fever at Ecbatana and died so suddenly that, when he took a turn for the worst and Alexander had to be summoned from presiding over celebratory games, the king could not reach his friend in time to share a last word. When Alexander did arrive at Hephaestion's bedside to find he had breathed his last, the disconsolate king flung himself upon the body and lay there the whole day long, weeping, refusing to be separated from his companion until his marshals dragged him away by force. For days thereafter, the heartbroken Alexander took no food or drink, nor spoke to anyone, except

Facing page: **Soldiers paying final tribute to the dying Alexander the Great in Babylon, 323 BCE.**

perhaps to order Hephaestion's doctor, Glaucias, hanged, either for having given his friend the wrong medicine or for making no attempt to keep him from drinking too much once the fever had afflicted him. But Alexander's rage was not limited to mere human beings. He ordered Ecbatana's temple of Asclepius, the god of medicine and healing, razed to the ground without delay. If the god could not save his dearest friend, what good was he? Alexander commanded that sacrifices, henceforward, be made to Hephaestion as a demi-god and the great tomb he built for him at Babylon cost upwards of 10,000 talents.

Death at Babylon

Alexander was not the same after Hephaestion's death. He grew colder, troubled, withdrawn; his former unquenchable passion and enthusiasm fizzled. He managed to conduct one last successful campaign against the Cossaeans before settling down at Babylon, perhaps his intended administrative capital, where he hoped to busy himself with the restoration of Bel-Marduk's ziggurat and temple, a project he had ordered begun seven years earlier, at the time of his first visit. We are told that Alexander contemplated an expedition against Arabia. He went so far as to send ships to scout the Arabian coastline. They returned with ample intelligence, although one fact struck Alexander most pointedly. The Arabs, it was said, worshipped two gods only, Uranus and Dionysus, the latter because of the fame of his journey to India. Alexander responded that it would not be beyond merit for the Arabs to worship him as a third god since 'his achievements surpassed those of Dionysus' (Arrian, VII.20).

In early June 323 BCE, Alexander, as was his custom, drank deep into the night with friends. The next day, he was not able to rise from his bed. Within a week, on 11 June 323 BCE, Alexander 'the Great' was dead. The cause of his death remains one of history's great mysteries. Many possibilities have been identified, among them: malaria, typhus, lingering complications or infection from the chest wound he received against the Mallians, and, of course, poisoning. He had travelled long and far, suffered many and significant wounds, was a heavy drinker and was known to be somewhat careless with regard to his own health, whether he was plunging recklessly into frigid waters before the city of Tarsus, riding at the very apex of his great cavalry wedge, or demanding to be first over some fortress wall. His illness was, however, characterized by high fever and some measure of paralysis, which seems to have intensified over time, symptoms that could well be characteristic of poison, but of other maladies as well. The question of poisoning inevitably leads to another question: who stood to benefit most by Alexander's death? And if the events that followed Alexander's passing are any indication, that is a very tricky and difficult question to answer.

What is more relevant is the fact that led directly to the disintegration of Alexander's empire at his death: his failure to bear or name a living heir before he lay on his deathbed. True, Roxane was pregnant with his unborn child, but the pregnancy would come far too late to save Alexander's empire. Antipater and Parmenion had urged him to take a wife and to father a son even before he had left Macedon 11 years earlier, but at that time he had no interest in such things. Perhaps his mind had not changed, even as he took his last breaths. Perhaps, as his commanders gathered round his bed, he was, possibly for the first time since Hephaestion's death the old Alexander again, for when they asked him to whom he would leave his kingdom, he replied simply, 'To the strongest' (Arrian, VII.27).

Right: A wood engraving depicting the funeral procession (and sarcophagus) of Alexander at Babylon, 323 BCE.

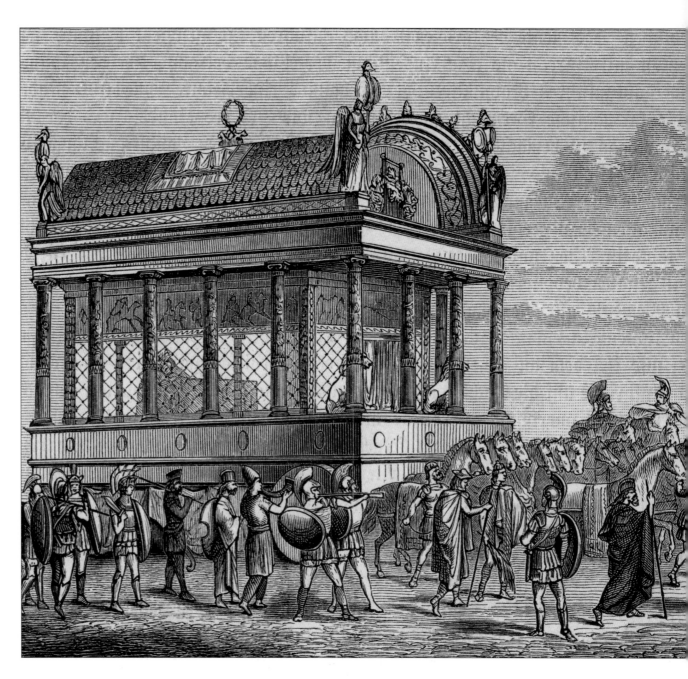

Alexander's Cities

Alexander saw in Egypt and Babylonia the greatest prizes of the Persian Empire. They linked the line of Cyrus to a storied and radiant past, to Djoser and Hammurabi, to Memphis, Thebes, Sumer and Akkad, to the natural and material wealth of the Nile and the Euphrates, to the birthplaces of empires, to the cradles of civilization itself.

A lexander and the Greeks knew well the historical pedigree of the two great river valley civilizations. Herodotus had devoted the entire second book of his *Histories* to Egypt. For Alexander, a passionate observer of the mythic past, the history of these places was their primary allure and he consistently paid homage to that history and the culture(s) that grew out of it. The Great King of Persia's interest in them was likely more mundane. Egypt and Babylonia were the wealthiest and most densely populated Persian satrapies. They were also administrative nightmares, at least for the Persians.

Facing page: This bronze statue on a marble base shows Alexander the Great sitting astride his horse, Bucephalus, in Thessaloniki, Greece.

Right: Head of Zeus-Ammon with ram's horns from Egypt, a Roman copy of a Hellenistic original. Now displayed in the Brooklyn Museum, New York.

The very history and prosperity that made them boons of conquest also made them difficult to control. Babylon had revolted in 522 BCE with such savage determination that, even before Darius I could lay siege to the city, her male inhabitants rounded up and strangled all unnecessary women in order to keep them from consuming the limited foodstuffs (Hdt. III.150).

Babylonian zealotry paid off for a time. Only by the ruse of the equally zealous Persian officer, Zopyrus, was the city taken after a siege of nearly two years. The dedicated Zopyrus had infiltrated the city by claiming to be a deserter from the army of the Great King. To ensure that the Babylonian rebels would believe him, he cut off his own nose and ears, blaming the cruel deed on Darius. In 486 BCE, the city rebelled again, this time claiming that Xerxes was out to obliterate worship

Above: This fifth-century BCE limestone relief from Persepolis shows the Great King, Darius I (r. 522–486 BCE), seated on a throne with crown prince Xerxes and attendants.

of the high god Bel-Marduk in Mesopotamia. The uprising dragged on for almost four years, but the Persians prevailed at last and Marduk – or at least his cult statue – was hauled off to Persepolis as Xerxes' prisoner. Egypt had more recently troubled the Great King. For some 60 years, rebel pharaohs had controlled the Nile Valley before Artaxerxes

III 'Ochus' (r. 358–338 BCE) and the Persians recaptured it in 343 BCE.

In the opening act of the re-occupation, Artaxerxes reportedly killed the sacred Apis bull of Memphis, just as Egypt's last Persian conqueror, Cambyses (r. 530–522 BCE), son of Cyrus the Great, was said to have done, mocking the priests of Apis as he did so (Hdt. III.27–29): 'You call *that* a god, you poor creatures?' As with Xerxes' unceremonious treatment of Marduk, the slaying of the Apis bull sent a symbolic message. The Great King would

not tolerate disloyalty, not even if the gods had encouraged it.

Alexander's 'Localizing' Foreign Policy and Appreciation of the Mythic Past

It is surprising, then, that the people of Egypt and Babylon, who had so long bridled under the yoke of Persian occupation, welcomed *another* conqueror, Alexander of Macedon, with open arms. This raises an important but sometimes overlooked fact about the political situation Alexander encountered as he gobbled up the former Achaemenid Empire. Alexander did not just found cities or, in some cases, glorified military colonies. He inherited cities from his Persian predecessors. These existing cities were culturally diverse foundations: Greek, Phoenician, Phrygian, Syrian, Babylonian and Egyptian, among others. Almost all of the cities that Alexander actually founded lay east of the Tigris River, Alexandria in Egypt being a notable exception. The reason for this is a quite practical one. Between the Aegean Sea and the Tigris, there already existed a wealth of thriving cities, occupying areas of strategic, commercial or ritual importance. Even in the case of Alexandria in Egypt, Alexander had not entered an unknown, uninhabited and certainly not unproblematic region of the world, even if the precise site near the northwestern banks of Lake Mareotis had been heretofore unsettled. Alexander's reception by and behaviour toward the existing cities of Asia Minor, Syria, Egypt and Mesopotamia represents an important starting point for exploring the 'cities of Alexander'. For many of these cities bore richly-tapestried mythic pasts, upon which their peoples clung and for which their peoples fought, be it Persia or some other would-be outsider conqueror.

And yet the indigenous peoples of a land as ancient and celebrated as Egypt thronged to the

Right: Alexander and his army enter Egypt, welcomed by throngs of cheering locals, with the Great Sphinx of Giza depicted in background. (From a nineteenth-century magazine illustration.)

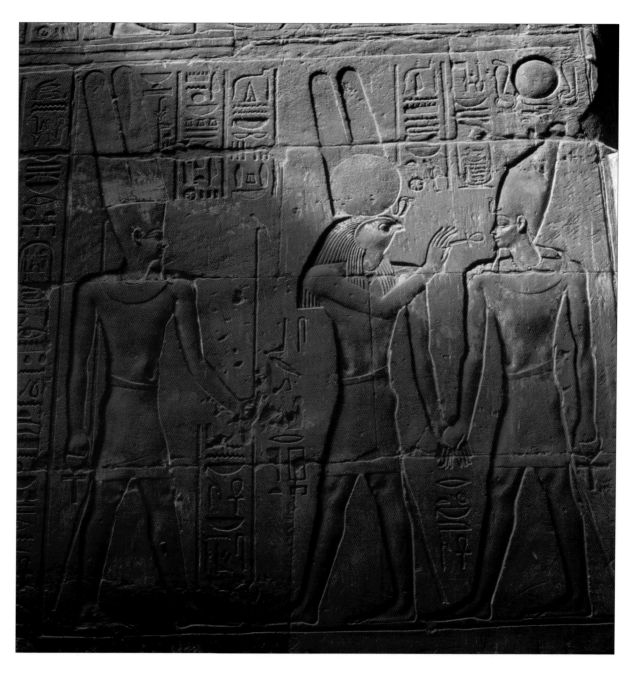

great fortress of Pelusium, on the eastern edge of the Nile delta, where Alexander first entered their territory, to welcome him as hero and liberator. Had a reputation for benevolence preceded him? Did Alexander and his Graeco-Macedonians share some connection to the peoples of Western Asia that the Persians did not? Was Persian rule so deeply unpopular that *anybody* other than the Great King would have enjoyed a warm reception? All of these factors contributed to the Macedonian king's welcome. But Alexander's own actions played a large role as well. Alexander seized upon – indeed paid homage to – the religious symbols, oracles and myths of nearly every city he conquered. At first glance, Alexander's behaviour appears as ingenious propaganda and the king himself, as a calculating politician, determined to win the loyalty of his new subjects by portraying himself as the antithesis of a remote and intolerant Persian king.

Whereas Achaemenid kings had slain the Apis bull, Alexander offered Apis special honours amid the sacrifices and games he held to celebrate his triumphal entry into Egypt in the winter of 332/331 BCE and made a point to visit the funerary temple at

Left: Wall relief, inner sanctuary, Temple of Luxor, depicting Amun-Ra (left), and Horus (centre), passing the *ankh* ('key of life') to an unidentified pharaoh, sometimes equated with Alexander. Luxor, Egypt.

Facing page: The extent of Alexander's empire by 325 BCE. Crossed-swords indicate locations of major battles. The red route lines suggest the probable course of Alexander's long march.

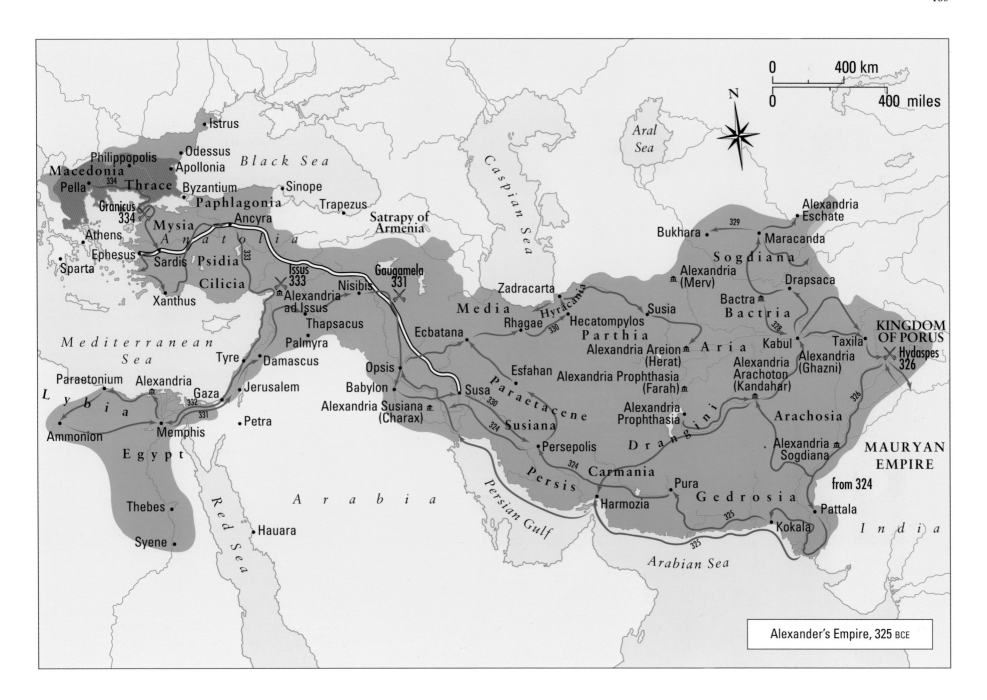

• Istrus

Black Sea

Macedonia
Philippopolis
• Odessus
Pella
• Apollonia
334
Thrace
• Byzantium
• Sinope
Granicus
Paphlagonia
• Trapezus
334
Ancyra
Satrapy of
Mysia
Armenia
A n a t o l i a
Athens
Sardis Psidia
333
Ephesus
Gaugamela
Sparta
Cilicia
Issus
331
Nisibis
333
Xanthus
Alexandria
ad Issus
Media
Zadracarta
Thapsacus
Rhagae
Hyracania
Susia
Palmyra
Ecbatana
330
Hecatompylos
M e d i t e r r a n e a n
Parthia
S e a
Tyre
Alexandria Areion
Damascus
(Herat)
Paraetonium
Opsis
Esfahan
Alexandria
Alexandria Prophthasia
Libya
Babylon
Susa
(Farah)
Jerusalem
Gaza
Paraetacene
332
Alexandria Susiana
Alexandria
Ammonion
331
(Charax)
330
Prophthasia
Memphis
• Petra
Susiana
324
Egypt
Persepolis
Drangini
A r a b i a
Persis
324 Carmania
Thebes
Pura
Persian Gulf
Gedrosia
Hauara
Harmozia
325
Red Sea
325
Arabian Sea

Aral Sea

Caspian Sea

Alexandria
Eschate
Bukhara
329
Maracanda
Sogdiana
Alexandria
(Merv)
Drapsaca
Bactra
Bactria
328
Aria Kabul
Taxila
KINGDOM
OF PORUS
Alexandria
Alexandria
(Ghazni)
Hydaspes
Alexandria
326
Arachoton
(Kandahar)
326
Arachosia
Alexandria
Sogdiana
MAURYAN
EMPIRE
from 324
Pattala
Kokala
I n d i a

Alexander's Empire, 325 BCE

Saqqara, where the mummified remains of deceased bulls were venerated collectively as Osiris-Apis, lord of the underworld.

Indeed, Alexander rarely encountered a local myth to which he did not feel some personal connection; he rarely encountered a god in whom he did not see some semblance of his own divine patrons: Zeus, Athena, Heracles, Dionysus and Achilles. If, by this devotion, he might win the hearts of the peoples of Asia, the fact only bolstered his belief – or delusion – in his own destiny. Alexander's 'foreign policy' seems to have been based on his uncanny ability to find in local traditions a rationale for his divine mission and a reason for veneration. Make no mistake, Alexander sought to minimize the possibility of resistance whenever possible, to secure politically-expedient alliances and to march on to meet Darius in battle as quickly as possible, so he had good strategic reasons to maintain at least the administrative *status quo* in the cities he came to control, but was his pointed obeisance to local religious tradition necessary in all cases to win the affection and allegiance of the people of the cities?

Loosening the Gordian Knot

In spring 333 BCE, Alexander rendezvoused with Parmenion at Gordium, the ancient capital

Facing page: Early nineteenth-century illustration depicting the tomb of Midas, King of Phrygia, c. 738–695 BCE, the second of three members of the Phrygian royal house to bear the name Midas.

of Phrygia. Already he had demonstrated his inclination to leave the Persian system of satrapies in place. After the Battle of the Granicus (334 BCE), Alexander had not abolished the satrapy of Lesser Phrygia, but merely replaced the Persian satrap – the absentee Arsites, who had fled after the battle and later committed suicide – with one of his own appointees. In some instances, he did not even go this far. Upon reducing Lycia, Pamphylia and Phrygia, he changed little of existing administration. When he did, he had good reasons for doing so and the changes were almost always well received. At Ephesus, for example, he restored democratic institutions and transferred to the Temple of Artemis funds previously paid in tribute to the Great King. The Ephesians celebrated him for his gift to their patron goddess. In Caria, Alexander was met by Ada, sister of the dynast Mausolus, whom he reinstated as ruler of the satrapy merely because she had petitioned him in person. The Carians lauded him for his favour and Ada rewarded him by adopting him as her own son. Although he most often left civil administration in the hands of the locals, Alexander also left Macedonian military governors behind to ensure that local loyalties held firm.

At Gordium, a local relic caught the king's attention. Arrian tells us that Alexander could not resist the lure of a famous wagon, affixed to its yoke by an inseparable knot. Here, Alexander exhibited the *pothos* or enthusiastic longing that seized him so often during his Asian expedition. The knot, the current object of Alexander's enthusiasm, was so

ornately tied 'that no one could see where it began and where it ended' (Arrian II.3). At the very least, this would have represented a challenging puzzle to a man with an insatiable appetite for doing what others thought impossible. But the wagon's history and the tantalizing oracle connected to its knot made it much more. According to the prophecy, the man who could unloose the knot would become the master of all Asia. As to the wagon's history, it was said to be the very wagon in which Midas had arrived at Gordium, from whence he would bring to an end decades of civil strife among the Phrygians and be acclaimed king. The Phrygians saw in Midas the fulfilment of an oracle, which foretold the coming of a man in a wagon who would bring peace to their war-torn land.

The legend goes on to state that Midas consecrated the wagon as a thank-offering to Zeus, placing it on display in the palace on the city's acropolis. Macedonian tradition made Midas himself a former Macedonian who had migrated to Phrygia. Herodotus' report (VII.73) that the Phrygians (formerly called the Briges) once lived in Macedon and later emigrated to Asia certainly lends credence to the notion that such a tradition existed. If so, Alexander would have known the Midas tradition well. Further, his education by Aristotle took place in the precinct of the nymphs at Mieza, a sprawling suburb of rolling hills, orchards and vineyards, which lay in (or very near) the so-called 'Gardens of Midas'.

Therefore, when Alexander undid the Gordian Knot – either by a stroke of his sword or by simply

Above: Ruins of Gordium, the ancient capital of Phrygia (modern Yassıhüyük, Turkey).

of the knot's loosening revealed Zeus' approval of Alexander's action and confirmed the validity of the oracle. The next day, Alexander offered sacrifice in thanks for the sign. By untying the knot, Alexander paid homage to a local tradition and won the admiration of the residents of Gordium. That tradition, however, he imbued with a deep personal significance that extended to his Macedonian homeland and, more importantly, to the blessing of Zeus himself.

The Cicilian Gates and Tyre

After this propitious display at Gordium, Alexander advanced toward Ancyra in Galatia, where a deputation of Paphlagonians offered him submission and friendship. In Cappadocia, he received the capitulation of 'all territory bounded by the River Halys' without even threatening a blow. Here he confidently left the Persian satrap, Sabictas, in place and marched on to the Cilician Gates. Although a number of defenders held the Cilician Gates, they fled their posts at the news of Alexander's approach and Tarsus too was taken without a fight. In spite of hillside skirmishes around Soli, he held games there and allowed the town to retain its own government. At Magarsus, he made sacrifice to 'the local Athena', an act that once again would have both placed him in the good graces of the villagers and served his personal religious aspirations. Whether the Magarsian goddess was the same Athena to whom Alexander had dedicated his armour at Dascylium, the very patroness of his Asian expedition, we cannot know

removing the wooden peg around which the knot was affixed, depending on which tradition one accepts – he not only fulfilled a local Phrygian oracle. He was following in the footsteps of a fellow Macedonian, who had been blessed by Zeus with the throne of Phrygia and who had shown proper devotion to the god by dedicating the wagon to him thereafter. Thunder and lightning the night

The Gordian Knot

There was also another traditional belief about the wagon: according to this, the man who undid the knot which fixed its yoke was destined to be the lord of Asia. The cord was made from the bark of the cornel tree, and so cunningly was the knot tied that no one could see where it began and where it ended. For Alexander, then, how to undo it was indeed a puzzle, though he was nonetheless willing to leave it as it was, as his failure might possibly lead to public disturbances. Accounts of what followed differ: some say Alexander cut the knot with a stroke of his sword and exclaimed, 'I have undone it!', but Aristobulus thinks that he took out the pin – a sort of wooden peg which was driven right through the shaft of the wagon and held the knot together – and thus pulled the yoke away from the shaft. I do not myself presume to dogmatize on the subject. In any case, when he and his attendants left the place where the wagon stood, the general feeling was that the oracle about the untying of the knot had been fulfilled. Moreover, that very night there was lightning and thunder – a further sign from heaven: so Alexander, on the strength of all this, offered sacrifice the following day to the gods who had sent the sign proclaiming the loosening of the knot.

ARRIAN, *THE CAMPAIGNS OF ALEXANDER*, II.3

Above: Alexander inspects the famed Gordian knot before attempting to loosen it in this oil on canvas painting by Giovanni Paolo Pannini.

Below: The Cilician Gates, through which Alexander passed before taking the seat of the Persian satrapy (of Cilicia) and important trade centre of Tarsus.

for certain, but the gesture resonated with the locals all the same. At Mallus, Alexander remitted the town's tribute to the Great King on the grounds that Mallus was a colony of Argos, the homeland of his patron and ancestor, Heracles. Indeed, Alexander

seldom missed an opportunity to propitiate one of his divine protectors, no matter the form the god or goddess took. But to the inhabitants of Western Asia, he was honouring *their* gods on *their* terms. The Great King simply had not done the same.

Alexander's desire to propitiate local deities and pay homage to local customs did not always meet with local approval. At Tyre, the king wished to sacrifice to Melqart, whom Diodorus calls 'the Tyrian Heracles' (XVII.40.3). Arrian goes further, claiming that the sanctuary of Melqart/Heracles at Tyre was the most ancient shrine of Heracles in the known world (II.16). The Tyrians greeted Alexander's request with staunch opposition. The rebuff drew Alexander into the protracted siege of Tyre from January to July 332 BCE. The Tyrians perhaps had good reason to refuse Alexander. Tyre was the leading city of Phoenecia, privileged of the Great King. Alexander's request essentially forced the Tyrians to take sides, for allowing the Macedonian king the honour of sacrifice meant rejecting – at least ceremonially – their Persian benefactor. The point to be gleaned, however, is that once again we find the king of Macedon desiring to make sacrifice to a local god, Melqart, whom he saw as a manifestation of Heracles.

Alexander in Egypt and Babylon

So Alexander reached Egypt in the winter of 332/1 BCE to jubilant cries of liberation. Diodorus offers concrete reasons why: 'For since the Persians had committed impieties against the temples and governed harshly, the Egyptians welcomed

Below: The Cilician Gates, through which Alexander passed before taking the seat of the Persian satrapy (of Cilicia) and important trade centre of Tarsus.

the Macedonians' (XVII.49.II). As we have seen, Alexander commonly engaged local religious tradition along his march through Western Asia, but perhaps never to greater effect than here at Memphis in Egypt. As a final homage to the Egyptian gods, Alexander ordered the restoration of two temples (at Karnak and Luxor) that had likely been razed by Cambyses. In return for his beneficence, he was hailed as the legitimate successor to the pharaohs and duly invested with the traditional pharaonic titles: 'King of Upper and Lower Egypt, son of Ra, beloved of Amun'. It is true that these titles had been granted to the Persian kings as well, at least in a strict legal sense. But, if we can believe Pseudo-Callisthenes (I.34.2), the Egyptians gave Alexander a full-blown investiture ceremony in formal Egyptian fashion. Whether or not such a ritual took place, the titles conferred upon Alexander were freely given and they actually meant something. In the case of the Persian kings, they were nothing more than a legal formality granted under duress.

About this same time, Alexander became eager to visit the shrine of the Libyan Ammon at the Oasis of Siwah. It is important to note that, here again, we find Alexander seeking out a local deity, whom he (and many Greeks before him) believed to be a manifestation of Zeus. So obvious was the god's identification with the master of Olympus that Callisthenes, Alexander's court historian, could drop the local nomenclature altogether and refer to Ammon simply as 'Zeus'. Arrian reveals a further rationale for Alexander's wish to visit the

oracle. His ancestral patrons, Heracles and Perseus, had undertaken the same journey. Alexander would have been remiss not to follow in their giant footsteps (III.3–4). And follow in them he did. Whereas up to now, Alexander's religiosity had served him well, hereafter it would become a source of tension within his ranks as the king's piety drifted increasingly toward fanaticism.

After decisively defeating Darius' army at Gaugamela in 331 BCE, Alexander fixed his gaze on the great metropolis of Babylon. There, as in Egypt, he was greeted with rejoicing. Before the walls of the city, Mazaeus – the Persian satrap who led Darius' right wing at Gaugamela – and representatives from the priesthood of Bel-Marduk (the so-called *Chaldeans*) met the king of Macedon. They placed the city unconditionally in his hands. The Babylonians insisted that Alexander enter the city in triumphal procession and he happily obliged them. Again he showed himself the antithesis of his Persian predecessors.

Whereas Xerxes had removed Marduk's cult statue and destroyed his temple, Alexander made formal sacrifice to the god and ordered that his temple at Esagila be restored. In addition, Alexander took the advice of Marduk's priests in all matters of religious ritual, which surely included the investiture ceremony that formally pronounced him Babylon's king. If the love-fest between Alexander and the Babylonian priests did not last, it was not for the

Right: Columns and bases from the Temple of Melqart, Tyre, can still be seen today.

king's lack of effort. He might have displayed a rare insensitivity to local religious tradition by ordering that funds from the temple treasury – funds whose use belonged exclusively to the purview of the priests and *not* the king, Macedonian, Persian or otherwise – be used for rebuilding the Temple of Marduk, but otherwise he assiduously played the role of Babylonian king. In the eyes of some in the Macedonian army, it was a role that Alexander played all too well. Alexander is commonly called 'orientalizing' in his approach to governance from his arrival at Babylon forward, but he had been 'localizing' in his approach to the cities and peoples he had contacted all along his way, and it would seem that he simply followed the same trend when he reached the Euphrates Valley's greatest city.

To take Alexander's historians at face value, one would have to conclude that the king of Macedon never met a god whom he did not like. He never found an oracle unworthy of consultation. He never encountered a myth that did not merit investigation. One wonders how Alexander had so much time for religion. He was, after all, in the midst of a campaign to take down the mighty Achaemenid Empire. One wonders if there was any logic behind the king's behaviour. Logic quite possibly was the furthest thing from Alexander's mind. He was either

Left: Alexander pays homage to the sacred Apis bull at Memphis (Egypt) in anticipation of performing a sacrifice.

Facing page: Alexander's triumphal procession through the streets of Babylon by eighteenth-century artist Gasparo Diziani (Musee des Beaux-Arts, Dijon, France).

deeply, sincerely – perhaps fanatically – religious or so politically astute an observer of history that he capitalized on Persia's religious insensitivities by acting in diametrical opposition to them. Maybe he was a bit of both. One point is certain. Alexander's devotion or political manipulation served him superbly throughout his conquest of the Persian West. Indeed, if religious fervour helped him fulfill the Oracle at Gordium, it would likewise prove to be his undoing. But now that we have seen Alexander's approach to the existing cities he encountered on his great march, let us examine some of the cities he and his successors founded, beginning with the one that would soon become one of the greatest of all ancient metropolises: Alexandria in Egypt.

The Return of the God-king

Indeed, Alexander and his successors quite literally transformed the Near East by founding cities, urban centres that would play a critical role in the so-called 'Hellenistic' period (323–31 BCE) that preceded Rome's ultimate domination of the Mediterranean world. It is important to recognize that the adjective 'Hellenistic' (although derived from the archaic Greek term 'Hellene', meaning, effectively, 'Greek') here entails something more nuanced than just 'Greek'. It would be wrong-headed to talk about the period from the death of Alexander to the victory of Rome as the 'Greek' period, for

Facing page: Workers depicted restoring and rebuilding the Temple of Bel-Marduk (the city's patron deity) at Babylon, at the instigation of Alexander.

in it grew and flourished a society and *ethos* that, while ostensibly governed by 'Greek' kings and 'Greek' ideas, to a significant degree incorporated elements of indigenous culture and tradition as well, especially in the great melting-pot cities that arose after Alexander, places like Alexandria and Antioch. The Hellenistic age bore a markedly cosmopolitan profile that both hearkened back to the great river

Below: Ruins of Alexandria, Egypt. Little of the ancient city has survived into the present, with much of it being underwater.

Left: Alexander, in full battle regalia, leads a cavalry charge. His leopard-skin saddle pad represents a nod to Dionysus, a god for whom the leopard is a sacred animal.

civilizations of the ancient Near East with their god-kings, majestic cities and ritual extravagances and pointed forward to a newly commercialized and highly interwoven Mediterranean that connected Italy all the way to India's Hindu Kush mountains and even beyond. This is perhaps the most enduring facet of Alexander's legacy and it is most visible in the cities that he and his successors established. Alexander is reported to have founded some 70 of them, although the number may be exaggerated. His Seleucid successors established something on the order of 60 new cities from western Anatolia to Iran. These cities became conduits not only for the diffusion of Greek culture and its blending with native tradition, but centres of commerce, military outposts and hubs for local and long-distance trade. Cities both new and old likewise played vital roles as religious centres in the Hellenistic period as ruler cults fused respective kings with local religious symbolism and ideology. The joining of king to city was a fitting marriage. These two were, after all, the primary elements of Hellenistic society.

Alexander blazed the trail on all fronts. He set the model of kingship that his successors: the Ptolemies (in Egypt and, on occasion, Syria, Cyprus, southern Anatolia and the Aegean), Seleucids (Syria and western Anatolia to Afghanistan) and Antigonids (Macedon and the Greek mainland) would follow. Alexander made the bearing, appearance and person of the king – sometimes to the chagrin of his fellow Macedonians – central to royal ideology. His successors emulated his wearing of the Persian diadem, his willingness to lead troops personally into battle, even his use of the term *basileus* ('king'), a word that was used freely in Macedon but was both peripheral and somewhat taboo in the larger Greek world before Philip. Kingship became a mighty symbol of power, but the Successors would not be able to rule Alexander's far-flung empire by merely inspiring awe in their subjects. Ptolemy (d. 283 BCE), Seleucus (d. 281 BCE) and, at least briefly, Antigonus the One-Eyed (d. 301 BCE) faced the daunting task from which an early death had liberated Alexander. The successors seized upon locations where an administrative centre could be forged to the mythic past and blended with the geographical, cultural and political realities of the present, while serving as gateway to a new Hellenized future.

Alexandria: Jewel of the Mediterranean

Alexander's city foundations set the bar for his successors, especially his founding of the greatest Hellenistic city, Alexandria, in 332/1 BCE, a city that, under the Ptolemies, superseded the Pharonic capital of Memphis just as Greek culture superseded everything around it. Alexandria in Egypt was the first city the Macedonian conqueror founded on his long march. It has been said that here, between

Right: Alexander and his architect, Deinocrates, discuss the construction and layout of Alexandria, Egypt.

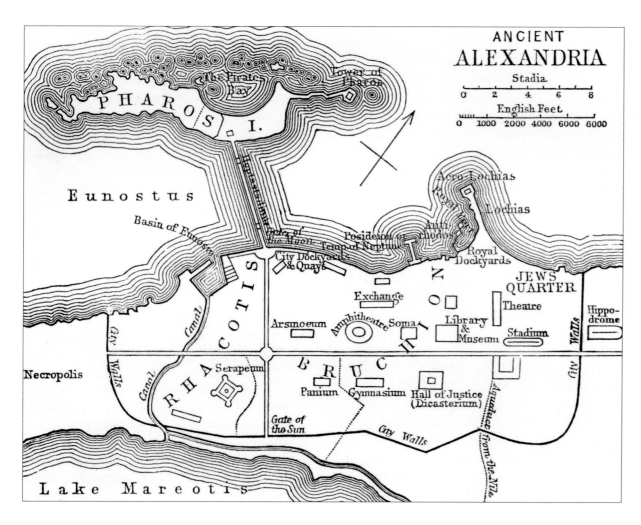

Above: Civic plan of ancient Alexandria in relationship to Lake Mareotis (bottom) and Pharos Island (top).

Lake Mareotis and Pharos Island, adjacent to a middling Egyptian fishing village called Rhacotis, Alexander himself, accompanied by the Greek architect Deinocrates of Rhodes, literally traced the circuit of the city. Because chalk could not be found, Alexander drew the city's boundaries with barley meal. Perhaps he intended it to be his own

ceremonial world capital, a great, bubbling cauldron that fused Greek, Egyptian and Persian cultures, Alexander's version of Achaemenid Persepolis. Although he chose precise locations for the city's *agora* (the civic centre and marketplace) and temples to Greek gods, he also transferred nearby Canopus' Emporium (trade centre) to Alexandria and offered the Egyptian residents of Rhacotis and Canopus privileged status for re-locating to the new city, another example of Alexander's localizing and inclusive politics. Even as river birds gobbled up the dropped pieces of meal and the superstitious Alexander despaired the dark omen, the king's seers assured him that the city there founded would have 'most abundant and helpful resources and be a nursing mother for men of every nation' (Plutarch, *Life of Alexander*, XXVI.8–10).

The nearby island of Pharos provided for the building of a large, deep-water outer harbour at the site, sheltered from the sea, and Lake Mareotis offered the prospect of an inner harbour, insulated from the massive barrage of silt carried annually down the Nile. Alexander's engineers would eventually join Pharos Island to the mainland via the Heptastadion, a large causeway measuring seven stades (furlongs), and the Ptolemies would build there one of the Seven Wonders of the Ancient World, the Lighthouse of Pharos, which towered some 130m (425ft) above the great harbour. Cunning Alexander likely realized, or was at least advised of, these strategic and commercial advantages of the city's would-be location. At the insistence of Deinocrates, or perhaps of Alexander

The Foundation of Alexandria

'Accordingly, he (Alexander) rose up at once and went to Pharos, which at that time was still an island, a little above the Canobic mouth of the Nile, but now it has been joined to the mainland by a causeway. And when he saw a site of surpassing natural advantages (for it is a strip of land like enough to a broad isthmus, extending between a great lagoon and a stretch of sea, which terminates in a large harbour), he said he saw now that Homer was not only admirable in other ways, but also a very wise architect, and ordered the plan of the city to be drawn in conformity with this site. There was no chalk at hand, so they took barley-meal and marked out with it on the dark soil a rounded area, to whose inner arc straight lines extended so as to produce the figure of a chlamys, or military cloak, the lines beginning from the skirts (as one may say), and narrowing the breadth of the area uniformly. The king was delighted with the design; but suddenly birds from the river and the lagoon … settled down upon the place like clouds and devoured every particle of the barley-meal, so that even Alexander was greatly disturbed at the omen. His seers, however, exhorted him to be of good cheer, since the city here founded by him would have most abundant and helpful resources and be a nursing mother for men of every nation, and so he ordered those in charge of the work to proceed with it, while he himself set out for the temple of Ammon.'

PLUTARCH, *LIFE OF ALEXANDER*, 26.7-10

Above: Alexander depicted designing the plan of the city of Alexandria in 331 BCE. His architect, Deinocrates, holds the map and advises.

PHAROS

Facing page: Illustration of the Lighthouse of Pharos (Alexandria, Egypt), one of the Seven Wonders of the Ancient World.

himself, the city was laid out on an axial grid so that her streets were well-positioned to receive the cool breezes that blew in from the Mediterranean. A kind of hinge between Africa and Europe, Alexandria would become the Mediterranean's most important port city and a bustling, cosmopolitan cultural centre to boot, a polyglot megalopolis, arguably the first city of its kind, at least in the European sphere. Alexander left no military complement at Alexandria, a fact suggesting that the king's prime interest for his first foundation was commercial and cultural. Even during Alexander's lifetime, Cleomenes, the king's finance minister and Alexandria's first governor, had already managed to make the city the hub of the Mediterranean grain trade. By 326 BCE, Alexandria had her own mint and a virtual trade monopoly, based on her prime location and the shrewd leadership of Cleomenes.

Ptolemaic Alexandria

Most telling, perhaps, is the fact that, having been allotted the satrapy of Egypt in the wake of Alexander's death, Ptolemy I wasted no time passing over the much older and storied city of Memphis for the shining new port city of Alexander's vision, a city founded less than a decade earlier. Here, Ptolemy brought and brilliantly displayed Alexander's embalmed body, stolen from the unfortunate Perdiccas, in a glistening coffin of gold.

Here, that same Ptolemy would collect the ancient world's most celebrated literary, religious and scientific writings and works of art and erect, for their keeping, the venerable Library and Museum of Alexandria. Ptolemy's project to preserve, protect and promote the great creative and scientific achievements of earlier Greek culture built upon the work of Aristotle's Lyceum and Plato's Academy, but it surpassed them both in magnitude and scope. The Ptolemies were insatiable in their desire to acquire texts for the library and archives. They had gone so far as to filch the master copies of Aeschylus, Sophocles and Euripides from the Athenians and they implemented a policy that those who arrived with scrolls must allow them to be copied before departing with them. Through these and other means, they may have ultimately accumulated more than 500,000 volumes.

Demetrius the Athenian, a pupil of Aristotle, had found his way to the new Egyptian city and may have consulted the Ptolemies on the building and layout of the grand facility. This, the world's

Left: Portrait bust of Ptolemy I 'Soter' ('Saviour'), ruler of Egypt (r. 323–283 BCE). Ptolemy wears the royal diadem, the formerly Persian symbol of kingship, which, after Alexander, was appropriated by the Successors. Louvre, Paris.

greatest shrine to the Muses (the divine beings from whence the Greek *mouseion* and, by extension, our English 'museum' is derived), grew into the world's foremost cult centre of education, surrounded by residence buildings for visiting students, scholars, philosophers and scientists, buildings for the library's vast holdings, halls for research and teaching and gardens for afternoon walks and, no doubt, lively conversation. In this idyllic, academic setting, Ptolemy would pen his own account of Alexander's conquests, although, like so many of Alexandria's precious volumes, it would not survive the wastes of time.

Ptolemy II 'Philadelphus' (r. 283–246 BCE) continued and expanded his father's work, fostering new scholarship in the Ptolemaic capital, including the translation of the Hebrew Bible into Greek in the form of the Septuagint, which catered to the city's massive Jewish population – many of whom had lost the ability to speak and read Hebrew – and would become the most important and influential version of Hebrew Scripture for Jews and Christians alike in the ensuing centuries. A cultural and educational hotbed and thriving commercial centre, Alexandria, less than 30 years after its foundation, already boasted a population of 100,000, a massive number by ancient standards. It would triple by the second century BCE. Alexandria was not only Alexander's 'first' city in practical application (i.e. founded during his Asian campaign), it was the city

Left: Ptolemy II 'Philadelphus' (283–246 BCE) depicted bringing new scrolls to the Library of Alexandria.

closest to Alexander's own mercurial and ingenious imagination and should rank among his greatest achievements, military, cultural or otherwise. Its grandeur would not be surpassed until Augustan Rome and, even then, not in all respects.

Other Alexandrias

The civic foundations of Alexander and his successors were commonly not located in previously urbanized areas; in fact, oftentimes, quite the opposite was true. Egypt's Alexandria had been founded near a rural fishing village (Rhacotis), although nearby Canopus bore some urban cachet. In the central Hindu Kush mountains, where the Valley of the Five Lions (the Panjshir) meets the Gorband, Alexander transformed a collection of meagre farming villages into a major centre of empire, Alexandria in Caucaso, by settling a core of 3000 Graeco-Macedonians and surrounding them with 7000 local farmers and herdsmen. Outside of Alexandria in Egypt, this arrangement was normative for the civic foundations of Alexander himself. The agriculturalist locals commonly outnumbered and largely supported the Graeco-Macedonian colonists, who themselves may not have readily embraced the life of would-be pioneers had their king not demanded it.

The marriage between colonist and indigenous folk was not always a happy one, but, in the case of Alexandria in Caucaso, the arrangement paid dividends. At a crossroads of the Hindu Kush, this Alexandria soon became important enough to have been enlarged by the king himself and it grew into a popular 'retirement' city for discharged soldiers. Even in ancient times, the Valley of the Five Lions was known to have been a bastion for the mining of precious gemstones, a fact that, along with its location, might have contributed to Alexandria in Caucaso's success. The king founded yet another Alexandria in Margiane (Merv), an important oasis in modern-day Turkmenistan and way-station on the ancient Silk Road. Although surrounded by one of the world's driest deserts (the Karakum),

Below: The Panjshir Valley (the 'Valley of the Five Lions') with Panjshir River (on the left) in the Hindu Kush mountain range.

the city would become a major trade centre, no doubt based on its favourable location along the great trade route and water access. Briefly, in the Middle Ages, the city was one of the largest in the world. But within some 50 years of Alexander's death, Alexandria in Margiane had already grown to such prominence that, by the early third century, Seleucid king Antiochus I (r. 281–261 BCE) thought it wise to rename it for himself. Thus it came to be called Antiocha in Margiane, though many locals continued to call it Alexandria. Other cities, like Alexandria Bucephala (named for Alexander's tireless horse, felled at the Hydaspes) and Alexandria Nicaea (the 'City of Victory'), erected on either side of the Hydaspes River, Alexander founded on the fringes of his empire, a kind of lawless no man's land where the lines between West and East blurred perhaps more than anywhere else in the orbit of the king's travels. These were likely intended to be defensive fortifications and they never became great cities. But great cities did arise in heretofore seemingly unimportant places.

Cities of the Successors

The city that Seleucus founded in 300 BCE and named for his son, Antiochus, was established in a sparsely-populated area on the Syrian coastal plain. It has been argued that the serene, majestic location of Antioch on a rolling plain sandwiched

Right: The Panjshir River near the Gorband, Hindu Kush. Alexander's army had to cross some very difficult terrain in their quest for world domination.

So Many Alexandrias...

All the cities that we know Alexander founded along his march to India were named Alexandria. Even the city he named for his beloved horse, Bucephalus, was called *Alexandria* Bucephala, not *just* Bucephala. Why? Alexander was certainly not an unoriginal thinker. The promotion of his own name and legacy through the foundation of cities named for him was far more important than variety when it came to cities' names. Alexander founded cities that – he hoped at least – would last forever, carrying his name and fame forward into the ages. Below are a few of the Alexandrias we know of and their modern locations (some of which are debated or unknown). Some Alexandrias did last. Some went on to become great cities and some even remain so today; others have left little or no physical traces of their existence. Only one, however, still bears the name of Alexander.

Above: Mud brick ruins of Alexandria in Margiane (Merv, Turkmenistan).

Alexandria in Arachosia (Ghazni or, more likely, Kandahar, Afghanistan)

Alexandria in Ariana (likely Herat, Afghanistan)

Alexandria Bucephala (likely Jhelum, Pakistan)

Alexandria in Caucaso (Bagram, Afghanistan)

Alexandria in Egypt (Alexandria, Egypt)

Alexandria Iomousa (likely at junction of the Chenab and Indus Rivers, Pakistan)

Alexandria on the Jaxartes (Kyrgyzstan, Uzbekistan, precise location unknown)

Alexandria in Markarene (likely Makran region, near the Hingol River, southwestern Pakistan)

Alexandria in Margiane (Merv, Turkmenistan)

Alexandria Nicaea (perhaps Mong, Pakistan or, more likely, just south of modern Jhelum)

Alexandria on the Oxus or **Alexandria in Tarmita** (Termez, Uzbekistan)

Alexandria in Prophthaisia (Lake Hamun, Sistan, Iranian-Afghan border)

Alexandria Rhambacia (Bela, Pakistan)

Alexandria in Susiana (Charax, abandoned c. ninth century CE, modern Kuwait)

204

Right: Bronze bust of Seleucus I 'Nicator' ('Victor'), founder of the Seleucid dynasty and empire (r. 312–281 BCE). Museo Archeologico Nazionale, Naples.

between the Orontes River and soaring peaks of Mt. Silpios, may have been precisely the reason for the choice of site. Here again, as with Alexandria in Egypt, location was everything. Perhaps unlike at Alexandria, however, the decision to situate Antioch in a highly defensible location may have had more to do with strategic concerns than commercial ones. Alexander's successors had warred with one another relentlessly after his death, ripping his empire apart and constantly reminding one another that one's hold on power could be exceedingly tenuous. The area was also a bastion of natural resources, its hinterland replete with incredibly rich and fertile soil; thick timber forests loomed nearby and fish from the coastal outlets were abundant. The Seleucids also liked to promote the notion that Alexander himself had mused upon the potential of the site, while passing through on his way to Egypt in 333 BCE. According to Libanius, he tasted the local spring water and compared it to 'mother's milk' (*Oration* 11). Even the torrential rains that pelted Antioch in winter and would have buried the city in topsoil, if not for some canny Macedonian engineering feats, did not dampen the city's prestige and the Seleucid commitment to constructing and promoting their own megalopolis on the Syrian

coast, a city that would nearly come to rival Alexandria in stature in the Hellenistic period. For the Seleucids, as for the Ptolemies, political success was inextricably bound to the power and profile of their chief city. After all, what was a Hellenistic king without a shining world capital?

Shameless self-aggrandizement of oneself or one's family members was a fixture of the Hellenistic age and capital cities with imposing locations were always helpful in this regard. Seleucus had been fond of re-telling the details of a dream wherein the deceased Alexander had stood beside him and acknowledged in no uncertain terms that he was destined to lead, to attain greatness 'as time went by' (Diodorus Siculus, XIX.90). And greatness in the successor kingdoms was germinated and grew in cities like Alexandria and Antioch. Even those cities that did not attain the heightened profile of the Hellenistic period's two greatest foundations bore the loftiest of ambitions, as was the case with the city of Uranopolis (literally, 'the City of Heaven'), founded by Alexarchus, son of Antipater, near holy Mt. Athos in Macedon. Alexarchus was even said to have created a new language for his heavenly city, although it almost certainly never found use outside its creator's own study and the occasional (and no doubt mystifying) letter he penned in it to his brother Cassander. Still, Alexarchus' high-minded

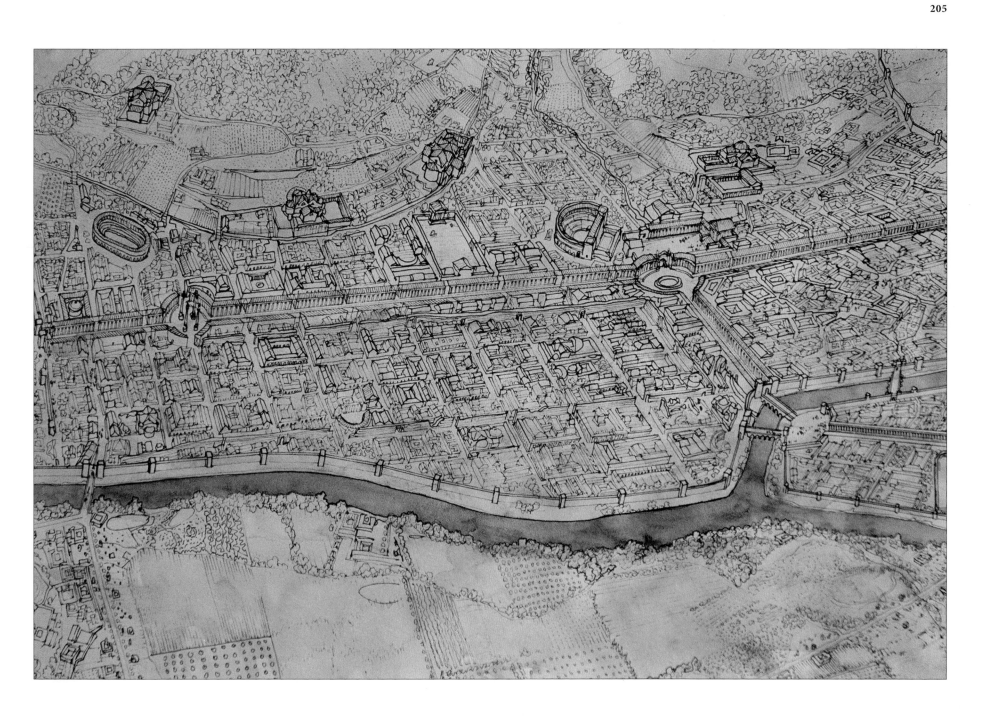

efforts are suggestive of the Successors' relentless pursuit of individual glory, achievement and prominence and of their deep desire to break new ground, to be 'founders' in their own right. Seleucus' son Antiochus I would try to mimic his father's feat by building his own Antioch near the Persian Gulf, but the city never quite matched the splendour of its predecessor. As Alexandria replaced Memphis for the Ptolemies, Seleucia on the Tigris replaced Babylon for the Seleucids.

Its location, 48km (30 miles) from the ancient Near East's most famous metropolis, potentially suggests a Seleucid wish to forge cities anew and on their own terms rather than to refashion existing urban centres. Together, the two cities exemplify the cultural dominance that the Successors imposed upon their subject peoples, even when those subject peoples (Egyptians, Babylonians) possessed celebrated legacies themselves. Indigenous cultures certainly coexisted beside Greek culture, with Egypt being perhaps the best example, but there was no doubt which culture was superior. Its will was imposed from the top down.

God-Kings

With cities came civic cult, most importantly, ruler cult. Whatever Alexander was told by the enigmatic Oracle at Siwah in 331 BCE, the quasi-divine

Facing page: Servants unload boats on ancient Antioch's waterfront. Antioch became a major commercial centre in the Hellenistic period (under Seleucid rule) and continued as such under the Romans.

Right: The Gonzaga Cameo, cut from three layers of Indian sardonyx. Third century BCE. It probably depicts Ptolemy II and Arsinoe, the Theoi Adelphoi ('Sibling Gods'), although Ptolemy II (foreground) is given the attributes of Alexander, a fact that has led some scholars to argue that the cameo depicts Alexander and his mother, Olympias.

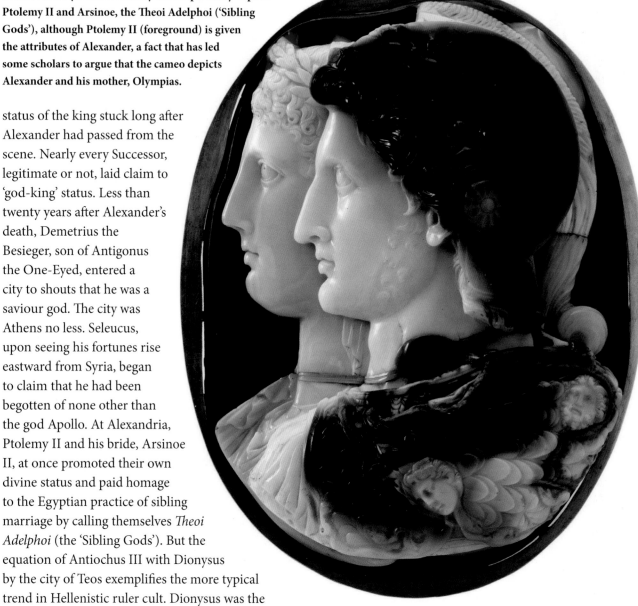

status of the king stuck long after Alexander had passed from the scene. Nearly every Successor, legitimate or not, laid claim to 'god-king' status. Less than twenty years after Alexander's death, Demetrius the Besieger, son of Antigonus the One-Eyed, entered a city to shouts that he was a saviour god. The city was Athens no less. Seleucus, upon seeing his fortunes rise eastward from Syria, began to claim that he had been begotten of none other than the god Apollo. At Alexandria, Ptolemy II and his bride, Arsinoe II, at once promoted their own divine status and paid homage to the Egyptian practice of sibling marriage by calling themselves *Theoi Adelphoi* (the 'Sibling Gods'). But the equation of Antiochus III with Dionysus by the city of Teos exemplifies the more typical trend in Hellenistic ruler cult. Dionysus was the

Above: Gold octadrachm (eight drachma piece) from Ptolemaic Egypt (c. 299–283 BCE), depicting Ptolemy I and his third wife Berenice I.

city's patron deity. The citizens of Teos essentially combined the attributes of the god with the king. Thus, Antiochus came to be associated with agriculture and fertility and his patronage of the city increased both yield and profit. The fact that Antiochus' statue was placed in the council hall where public business was transacted and propitiated there suggests the king's dual role as divine benefactor and royal administrator.

The Ptolemies in Egypt were happy to play the role of Pharaoh, as Alexander had been, and had themselves depicted as Pharaohs in Egyptian temples for exactly the same reason. The Pharaoh was already a god-king. A Ptolemaic king, as Pharaoh, then played the same role as an Antiochus fused with Dionysus. In some respects, the Hellenistic city looked backward as much as forward, to the theocracies of a bygone age: to Near Eastern precedents where kings ruled as deputies of the gods or gods themselves: to Nineveh, Babylon, Memphis, Uruk, even to Achaemenid Persepolis, where the Great King, the agent of the high god Ahura Mazda himself, hovered above his subjects like an extravagantly-ornamented and awe-inspiring avatar of heaven.

The coinage of the Successors commonly pointed up the equation of the kings with divine figures, but also, as the kings are most often depicted wearing the royal diadem, as successors to Alexander *and* the Great King of Persia. The Ptolemies became fond also of styling themselves with a radiate crown, or crown of the sun, which, in Egypt, could be seen as a nod to both the Egyptian sun god, Ra, and the Greek Apollo, yet one more example of the Hellenistic trend of cross-cultural pollination. Ptolemy III Euergetes (r. 246–222 BCE) added a trident to his gold octadrachm to pay homage also to Poseidon, the god of the sea, a fitting symbol for the Mediterranean's greatest port city.

A divine image or moniker, however, was not always a staple of Hellenistic coin types. The Seleucid 'elephant series', an example of which was minted from Ecbatana in the late third century BCE, proves that the power of the successor kings could be displayed and published in a quite this-worldly fashion. The coin bears only the image of Antiochus III wearing the diadem on the obverse with an elephant and the inscription 'King Antiochus' on the reverse. A *war elephant* to be precise, just like the ones that had served the Seleucid war machine at the decisive Battle of Ipsus in 301 BCE.

The equation of king with god was not always well-tolerated as Antiochus IV (d. 164 BCE) learned when he tried to force the issue in Jerusalem, an action that was met by the rise of wily revolutionary Judas 'the Hammer' and the Maccabean Rebellion. The Jews were not the only people to resist the

Facing page: The gates of Persepolis, the Persians' magnificent ceremonial capital, begun by the Great King, Darius I (522–486 BCE), completed by his son, Xerxes I (486–465), and burned by Alexander after an evening of drunken revels.

domination of the Successors and their mega-cities. Aratus and his Achaean League (280s–270s BCE) were bent on preserving 'the freedom of the Greeks' and resisting their Macedonian interlopers. The seven cities succeeded for a while, but eventually had to turn to Macedon for help against a surging Sparta.

Economics

It has been argued that the Successors had no real talent for money, especially when it came to the production and exchange of it, and the founding of new cities only marginally enhanced endemic production issues. The Ptolemaic economy collapsed in the second century BCE despite the fact that the kings were perched in the very bread-basket of the Mediterranean world. Egyptian papyri report enormous cargoes of grain in Alexandria's harbours, not to mention honey, oil and luxury goods. Some have argued that the Ptolemies became so bent on gluttonous excess that, even in the consumerist capital of the ancient world, the Alexandrian economy could not sustain itself.

Booty had been the name of the game in the course of Alexander's long march. Consider the fact that Alexander and his men had burgled the entirety of the Great King's treasure, in the form of gold bullion from Susa and Persepolis. In spite of the growth of permanent, even thriving, administrative

Right: Medieval manuscript rendering of Antiochus IV Epiphanes ('God Manifest'), ruler of the Seleucid Empire (175–164 BCE), riding triumphantly into Jerusalem, killing a few residents in the process.

and commercial centres, the acquisition of booty from conquered lands and peoples remained a constant, even a necessity, in the Hellenistic period. Among his other crimes, Antiochus IV filched 1800 talents from Solomon's Temple in Jerusalem. The Seleucid bureaucracy was less elaborate than the Ptolemies, a fact that forced them to devise ingenious schemes to keep the economic engine running. That meant lots of taxes (even on necessities like salt), levies and tribute and even a poll tax at Jerusalem. The Seleucids monopolized the production of gold and silver. This policy, apparently, kept them in abundant coinage, but did not avert the occasional need for the outright thievery of an Antiochus IV. One gets the sense that, financially speaking, the Successors were making it up as they went along.

Satellites of Hellenism

Still, the Hellenistic megalopolis and its institutions lay at the heart of the matter; they were the glue that *mostly* held the delicate balance of power together. These were the satellites that broadcast, legitimated, diffused and imposed the dominance of Greek culture after Alexander and created the cultural *koine* ('common tongue') that the Romans would ultimately inherit. But they also embraced indigenous cultural tropes and traditions and fostered a cosmopolitan consumerist model that would hold sway throughout the balance of Graeco-Roman antiquity. Here, as in much of their administrative activities, the Successors borrowed liberally from Alexander's playbook:

found a city, name it after yourself, promote the person of the king both on the field of battle and in marble, gold and silver, publish his power – but also his *benevolence* – at every turn and in every way possible. Like Alexander, they were often happy to leave present administrative structures in place, even as they attempted to carve out for themselves and their families their own enduring legacies and to supersede, with their own foundations, the history that preceded them, however celebrated that history might have been. The displacement of Memphis and Babylon by the Ptolemies and Seleucids, respectively, demonstrates this fact in clear relief. Like Alexander, the Successors fused

Above: Silver tetradrachm, Antiochus IV Epiphanes, wearing royal diadem. The eagle on the reverse is emblematic of Zeus and a symbol of kingship and power.

politics, religion, propaganda and military power to create a cultural hegemony that did not always pan out in the sphere of practical administration. The successors were not always loved or fully accepted by their subject peoples, perhaps unlike Alexander before them, but, as they jostled for power, resources and lands, they did forge a Mediterranean-wide cultural and commercial *koine* that was both Greek and more than Greek. Here, in the cities of Alexander and his successors, Hellenism was born.

The King is Dead. Long Live the King(s)

The story is told that, when Alexander realized his death was imminent, he stumbled from his bed and sneaked out of doors in the hope of throwing himself into the Euphrates. This way, he reckoned, he would simply disappear; his contemporaries and future generations would believe that he had left to take his place among the gods.

His wife, Roxane, caught him leaving the building, however, at which point he unleashed a great cry to heaven for denying him the 'eternal fame of divine birth' (Arrian VII.28). Whatever those who knew him – and posterity – may have believed about his divinity, about his everlasting fame, he need not have worried. His name and legacy would endure, even if the same cannot be said for his far-flung empire. More than two millennia removed from his death, his story, his accomplishments, his legend still haunt and captivate the human mind.

The Heated Debate over the Succession

Alexander's greatness, and everything the word entails, is best judged against the events that erupted in the immediate aftermath of his death. Most likely, the dying Alexander had given his signet ring – the symbol of his kingship – to Perdiccas, who became, with the passing of Hephaestion, the most trusted of his marshals. What was meant by the gesture?

Facing page: The Alexander Sarcophagus, with Alexander depicted (in lion headdress, an attribute of Heracles) fighting Persians at the far left of the side panel shown. The sarcophagus may have contained the remains of (or at least been dedicated to) Mazaeus, Alexander's former advisor turned ally and governor of Babylon.

Right: Marble statue of Alexander III of Macedon, (third century BCE), perhaps a copy of an original by Lysippus. Istanbul Archaeological Museum.

Arrian's Eulogy to Alexander

'Anyone who belittles Alexander has no right to do so on the evidence only of what merits to censure him; he must base his criticism on a comprehensive view of his whole life and career. But let such a person, if smear Alexander he must, first compare himself with the object of his abuse: himself so mean and obscure, and, confronting him, the great King with his unparalleled worldly success, master of two continents, who spread the power of his name over all the earth. Will he dare to abuse him then, when he knows his own smallness and the triviality of his own pursuits, which, even so, prove too much for his ability?

'It is my belief that there was in those days no nation, no city, no single individual beyond the reach of Alexander's name; never in the world was there another like him …'

ARRIAN, VII.30.

Roxane was perhaps six months pregnant with Alexander's much-delayed and hoped-for heir. Some reports suggest that Stateira (Barsine), whom Alexander had taken as his second wife at Susa, either had borne or was pregnant with a son also. As such, Alexander may have intended for Perdiccas to act as regent until his son(s) came of age. For his part, Perdiccas called a council of Alexander's commanders and 'returned' Alexander's ring, a calculatingly benevolent gesture that he hoped would win him the men's support for his position as the king regent (or king outright) and, if not, at least, lay the groundwork for a constructive debate.

It did neither. Immediately, Ptolemy spoke up and took exception to the notion that a son of Alexander's by Roxane or Stateira would ever be fit to rule, since he would be half-barbarian and 'mostly-slave.' (Curtius, X.13–14). Why, Ptolemy went on, should the Macedonians share the kingdom they were at such pains to conquer with descendants of the vanquished? At last, he proposed that matters of government should be decided by a committee, comprised of Alexander's chief generals. Perdiccas' supporters quickly objected to Ptolemy's proposal of rule by committee, but the cries that only a full-blooded Macedonian should rule continued to gain momentum.

The cavalry officer, Aristonus, argued that, if the king had passed his ring to Perdiccas, then Perdiccas should rule as king in his own right, but the battled-scarred general Meleager stepped up and accused Perdiccas of having engineered a sorry charade. Perdiccas' plan, he declared, was only to pretend to be regent, until the time was ripe for him to seize the throne for himself. At this point, as the din of raised voices echoed even louder and the debate began to rage out of hand, someone suggested that, in fact, the kingship should pass to Philip Arrhidaeus, Alexander's half-witted half-brother, the son of Philip and Philinna of Larissa. Meleager agreed and stood ready to support Arrhidaeus as king. Matters devolved from there. In the words of Curtius, 'No deep sea, no vast and stormy body of water produces waves as violent as the emotions of a mob, particularly in the first flush of a freedom that is to be short-lived' (Curtius, X.11).

The first conflict in the fight to divide the spoils of Alexander's conquests pitted Perdiccas against Meleager or, effectively, the Macedonian cavalry against the Macedonian infantry. Ultimately, many of the generals, including Ptolemy and Seleucus, sided with Perdiccas, but the belligerent Meleager and his infantry dug in their heels. Civil war appeared imminent. Perdiccas' cavalry contingent left Babylon, chased out of town by Meleager's threatening forces, and proceeded promptly to cut off supplies to the city and, by extension, Meleager's troops. Eumenes, Alexander's chief secretary, at last, managed to talk down the opposing sides by proposing a compromise that would allow Arrhidaeus and the unborn child – *if* the child proved to be a son – of Alexander and Roxane to rule as joint kings. The compromise bought Perdiccas time. With the child of Roxane born, a son indeed, and acclaimed Alexander IV, Perdiccas would soon find cause to have Meleager arrested and summarily executed.

With his position as regent apparently secure, Perdiccas summoned a council to Babylon to discuss the appropriate partitioning and governance of Alexander's empire. Almost all the key players were in attendance, except Antipater, who remained at Pella, Craterus, Alexander's choice to replace the aging viceroy of Greece, who had gotten as far as Cilicia when he heard of Alexander's death, and Antigonus the One-Eyed, whom Alexander had left as military commander of Phrygia, the guardian of precious supply and communication lines between Macedon and Greece and Asia Minor. The decisions of the council were telling, beginning with the reappointment of Antipater as master of Greece, apparently against Alexander's express wishes to the contrary. Craterus was the younger man, extremely popular among the infantry (a fact that may have led Perdiccas to contrive his marginalization), and Antipater had served his time, and proved a loyal soldier and friend to Alexander, despite dark rumours that he played some part in Alexander's death. It is difficult, indeed, to locate any possible motivation the respected Antipater, who neared the end of a long and decorated career in the service of Macedon, would have had to plot the assassination of Alexander.

We are fed stories that Olympias wrote to Alexander and expressed displeasure with Antipater's governance of Greece, letters that may have included charges that he was fomenting disloyalty to Alexander, but this too is hard to accept. Olympias may have found the old general quarrelsome in some respects, but it is hard to besmirch his loyalty to Alexander when all the facts are considered. Perdiccas' council threw Craterus a bone by making him guardian (*prostates*) of the two kings, Arrhidaeus and Alexander IV, but afforded

Below: Augustus, the first Roman emperor (r. 31 BCE – 14 CE), before the Tomb of Alexander III. Painting by Sebastian Bourdon (1616–1671), oil on canvas.

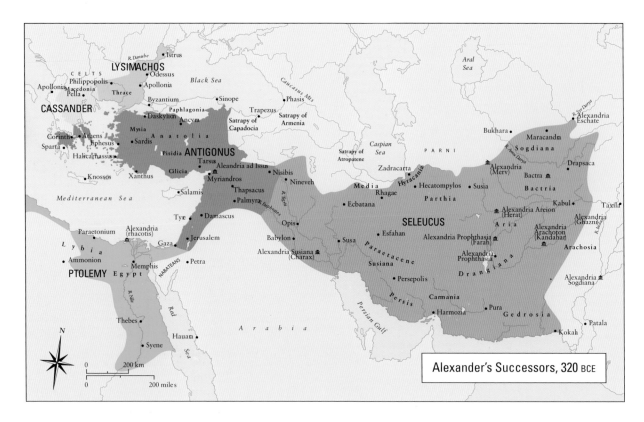

Alexander's Successors, 320 BCE

Above: Map showing the five-fold division of Alexander's former empire by 320 BCE into regions governed by Seleucus, Ptolemy, Antigonus the One-Eyed, Lysimachus and Cassander (the son of Antipater).

him little ability to exercise any real authority. Both kings resided at Babylon under the watchful eye of Perdiccas and the king regent would never deign to allow Craterus real access to them. In addition to Antipater, Ptolemy, Leonnatus, Lysimachus, Antigonus the One-Eyed and Alexander's secretary Eumenes, were all granted important appointments.

Notably absent from the list is Seleucus, who, for the moment, served as Perdiccas' right hand and was made supreme commander (*chiliarch*) of the Companion cavalry at Babylon. Ptolemy seems to have been almost alone among the successors in his understanding of the fact that success and longevity in the wake of Alexander's death would not be found in attempting to control all or even the largest portion of the gargantuan empire, but rather in selecting precisely the right piece of it. As such, he asked for and was granted appointment to the satrapy of Egypt.

By 319 BCE (not four years after Alexander's death), Perdiccas, Craterus, Antipater and Leonnatus were dead. The *Diadochoi* ('successors') had begun, almost immediately, to rip up the vast, hard-won empire, each of them firmly convinced that he was Alexander's rightful successor. The cleverest among them was Ptolemy, who had not only limited his ambitions to Egypt, but made a compelling case that Alexander would have wished to be buried there, at Alexandria, the king's most important civic foundation. Before Perdiccas had realized the value of holding on to the body of the deceased king, Ptolemy had snatched it and made considerable, propagandist hay by promoting the idea that his singular goal was to provide the fallen king with a glorious burial in the city he took pains to lay out near the banks of Lake Mareotis. Alexander was, by all rights, the successor of the pharaohs, Ptolemy argued. Once he had reached Alexandria with Alexander's corpse in tow, he would attempt, with some success, to make himself the same.

No True 'Successor'

None of the men who fought to command all or part of Alexander's empire were, in fact, true 'successors' to Alexander. Ptolemy's Egyptian kingdom survived the longest. Ptolemaic Egypt's last monarch, Cleopatra VII (d. 30 BCE), was only supplanted by Rome and, even then, it would take the Romans' finest politician and first emperor, Augustus, to do so. The dynasty founded by Seleucus, the only member of the *Diadochoi* to

remain married to the wife he took at Susa after Alexander's death, fared almost as well, falling to Pompey and those same Romans in 63 BCE. But, rather than focus on the shortcomings of these would-be successors, one must instead consider the extraordinary man they sought to succeed. Those very Macedonians, who had followed Alexander for more than a decade, many of whom had travelled with him across tens of thousands of miles, overcoming seemingly insurmountable odds, having attained the unimaginable in the process, instantly, upon his death, turned their swords on one another. It was not merely military or battlefield brilliance, infectious passion, charisma, irrepressible curiosity or the ability to inspire men to seek something larger than themselves that made Alexander great, although he surely possessed all these qualities and more. It was, finally, the sheer force of his indomitable will that spurred him on, even when the road ahead appeared dangerous and its end, unknowable. Herein lay his chief attribute. For his men had followed him, respected him and feared him because they sensed in him something prodigious and terrible. He had proved, time and again – at the crossing of a swelling river or the apex of a cavalry wedge or the acme of a fortress wall – that he seemed to lack the one paralyzing malady that all other mortal men possess: fear. In this, at least, Alexander walked with gods.

Left: A statue of Alexander the Great and Bucephalus today stands on a pedestal on Macedonia Square, the central square of the capital of Skopje, Republic of Macedonia.

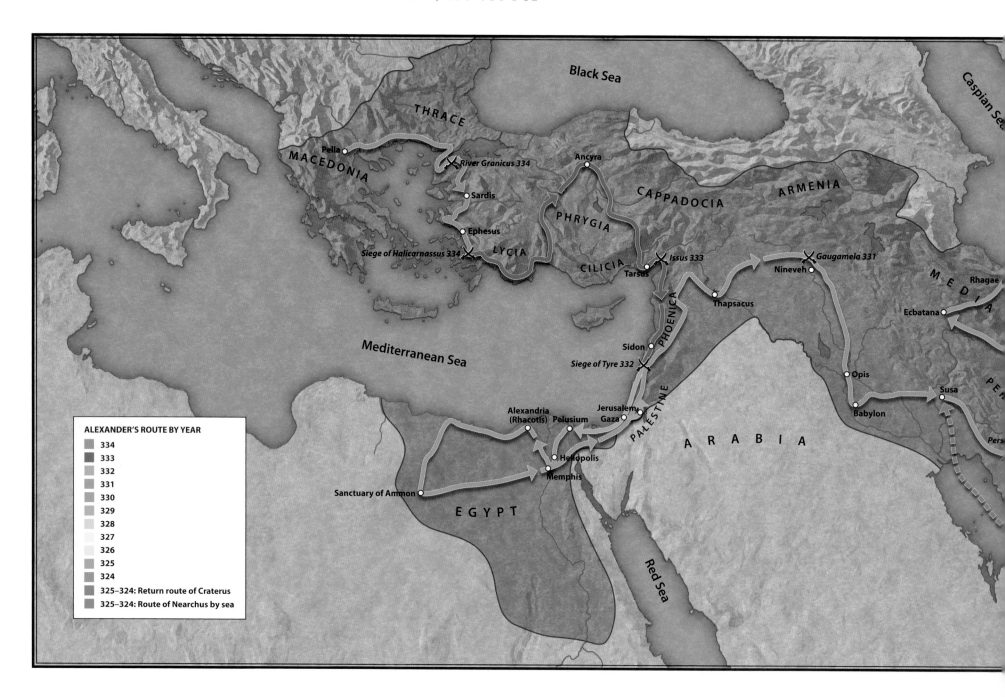

Black Sea

THRACE

MACEDONIA

Pella

River Granicus 334

Ancyra

CAPPADOCIA

ARMENIA

Sardis

PHRYGIA

Ephesus

LYCIA

Siege of Halicarnassus 334

CILICIA

Tarsus

Issus 333

Gaugamela 331

Nineveh

MEDIA

Rhagae

Thapsacus

Ecbatana

PHOENICIA

Mediterranean Sea

Sidon

Siege of Tyre 332

Opis

PALESTINE

Jerusalem

Babylon

Susa

Alexandria
(Rhacotis)   Pelusium

Gaza

Heliopolis

ARABIA

Memphis

Sanctuary of Ammon

EGYPT

Red Sea

Caspian Sea

PER

ALEXANDER'S ROUTE BY YEAR

334
333
332
331
330
329
328
327
326
325
324
325–324: Return route of Craterus
325–324: Route of Nearchus by sea

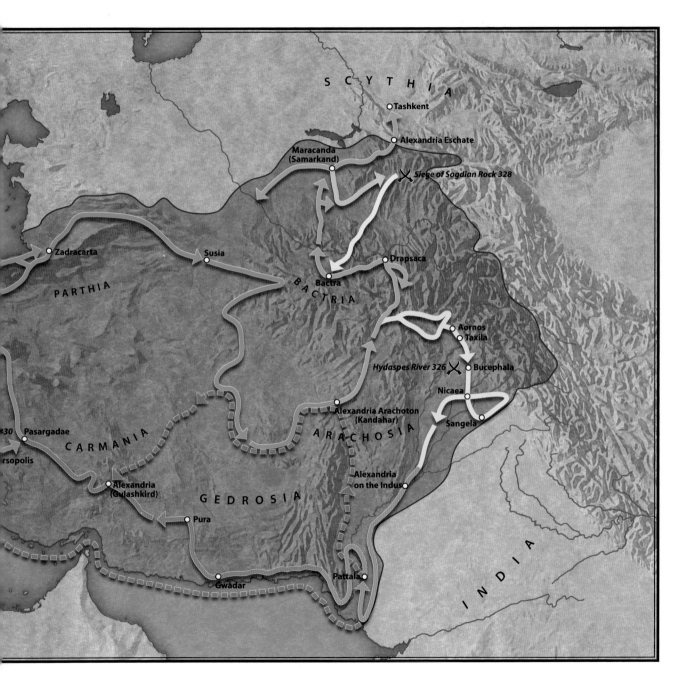

This map shows Alexander's probable route from Pella (in 334 BCE) to beyond the Indus and back toward Babylon through Gedrosia. Alexander's Asian campaign covered almost 24,140 kilometres (15,000 miles), mostly overland. Land travel was costly and difficult in the ancient world, especially for a large military force like Alexander's that required near-constant provisioning. Moving men and, especially, animals and supplies for even 30 kilometres (18 miles) along mostly rough, dirt roads (and sometimes no roads at all), made even less navigable by heavy rains, uneven topography or ice was as expensive and almost as time-consuming as travelling 1600 kilometres (1000 miles) by sea. Where proper roads did exist (e.g., the Achaemenid Royal Road), they were comprised of mixed cobblestone pavements stretching about five to seven metres (16–22 ft) wide, flanked by stone embankments – hardly ideal for a massive contingent of men, horses and baggage. Given the difficulties of ancient land travel, the distance and duration of Alexander's march alone represents an incredible achievement. Including his earlier campaigns in the Balkans and Greece, Alexander likely travelled upwards of 32, 200 kilometres (20,000 miles) in the course of his nearly 13-year reign, almost all of them overland, on foot or horseback.

How Do We Retell Alexander's Story? The Sources

Reconstructing the history of the ancient world is an exercise not unlike attempting to put together a jigsaw puzzle with most of the pieces missing. The historian's task, then, is to determine, based on what pieces remain, what once existed in the blank spaces in between. The evidence of Alexander's extraordinary life that endures today is a mere fraction of what once was; so much has been lost. Although we know that contemporaries of Alexander wrote accounts of his life and campaigns, not a single written source from Alexander's own lifetime survives intact. In fact, the earliest written source for Alexander's life, the seventeenth book of Diodorus Siculus' *Bibliotheca historica* ('Universal History'), was not penned until the mid-first century BCE, nearly 300 years after Alexander's death.

Closely following Diodorus, chronologically, was a Romanized Gaul named Pompeius Trogus, whose *Historica Philippicae* (named for Alexander's father, Philip II) only survives in the abridged version (or epitome) of Justin, a Roman historian writing sometime between the middle second and late fourth centuries CE. In the later first century CE (perhaps during the reign of Vespasian, 69–79 CE), the Roman historian Quintus Curtius Rufus wrote the only complete Latin account of Alexander's life and activity. His treatment was followed by that of the philosopher/biographer Plutarch of Chaeronea

(c. 50–120 CE) who wrote a biography of Alexander as part of his *Parallel Lives* (wherein he is paired with Julius Caesar) and wrote a moralizing take on Alexander's achievements and worldview in his *On the Fortune and Virtue of Alexander*. Lastly, Plutarch provides some information on Alexander in his *Sayings of Kings and Commanders*. Arrian's (c. 85–160 CE) *Anabasis Alexandrou*, written in the second century CE, is the final complete written source and is often considered by scholars to be the most useful – at least with regard to military matters. Although Arrian's book is apologetic in tone, scholars cite the fact that the author seems to get very specific details of battles and military engagements correct, suggestive perhaps that these passages are based on an eyewitness account of Alexander's campaigns.

In fact, many of the above sources appear to preserve elements of much earlier written records, some either from Alexander's own lifetime or from the pens of his contemporaries. Perhaps the most important of these is the account of Ptolemy, son of Lagus (c. 367–283 BCE), a member of Alexander's personal bodyguard and a major player in the wars that erupted in the wake of the Macedonian king's death. Arrian's *Anabasis* is largely based on Ptolemy's treatment, written from Alexandria, the newly-minted capital of Egypt's Ptolemaic Empire in the years that followed the Wars of the *Diadochoi*

('Successors'). Because Ptolemy was a member of Alexander's immediate retinue and played a sometimes significant role in his battles, especially during the Indian campaign, he would have been in prime position to recount the actual events on the ground. Ptolemy, however, was not the only contemporary of Alexander's to commemorate in writing the king's amazing exploits. Arrian also made use of the work of Aristobulus of Cassandreia (c. 375–301 BCE), an architect, engineer, geographer and close associate of Alexander, who accompanied the king for much of his long march. Aristobulus' work was not precisely a narrative account of Alexander's campaigns, but was principally concerned with geography and ethnography. Arrian, a military man who served as governor of Roman Cappadocia and commander of the Roman legions on the dangerous Armenian frontier, seems to have embraced the histories of Ptolemy and Aristobulus above all others or, perhaps, as some scholars have suggested, to the exclusion of all others. For Ptolemy and Aristobulus were not the only contemporary or near-contemporary sources to which Arrian would have had access.

Alexander himself had employed an official court historian to accompany him on campaign and memorialize his achievements. Callisthenes of Olynthus was a kinsman, perhaps the nephew, of

Alexander's tutor, Aristotle, and here again we would have an eyewitness account (even if coloured by Alexander's own biases) of the Macedonian king's career, although not all of it. Callisthenes ultimately came to be implicated in a plot to assassinate Alexander and likely died around 327 BCE. Nevertheless, threads, however faint, of Callisthenes' work are found in most of the surviving Alexander historians. Nearchus the Cretan, the admiral of Alexander's fleet and Onesicritus – who claimed to be an admiral, but was likely a mere helmsman in that same fleet – also wrote histories of Alexander, both apparently published in the immediate wake of his death. Callisthenes, Nearchus and Onesicritus were all employed by Cleitarchus of Alexandria, who wrote his history of Alexander at the court of Ptolemy in roughly the early third century BCE. Cleitarchus did not travel with Alexander on campaign, but his access to eyewitness accounts and reports as well as his father Dinon of Colophon's extensive history of the Persian Empire makes his work worthy of consideration. Cleitarchus' work became the most popular of all near-contemporary accounts of Alexander's life, perhaps because its author tended to sensationalize his subject and aggrandize events to serve his own dramatic storytelling purposes. For this reason, although Cleitarchus' own work does not survive, almost all Alexander historians seem to have had access to it and to have made use of it, in whole or part.

In sum, although we have no surviving written sources from Alexander's own lifetime, the sources that do survive all make use, to one extent or another, of sources directly contemporary to Alexander. All of these writers, however, whether they wrote in Alexander's day or at the height of the Roman Empire, had biases and agendas of one kind or another, to lift Alexander up, or tear him down, to carve him in the image of a philosopher king or Homeric hero or military-minded taskmaster or forerunner to the Roman achievement. As such, they must be read with caution and a critical eye. In the extant written sources, we find many Alexanders and sifting through the propaganda or mythology or individual preoccupations of the respective authors is no small task. But, if we utilize the written evidence judiciously, along with the material remains of Alexander's world, from coinage to weaponry to grave goods and beyond, I believe we can indeed uncover the 'real' Alexander, on his own terms and in his own time. For it is only then that the student of Alexander will understand, for well and ill, what it was like to walk in his 'great' footsteps.

Select Bibliography

Arrian. *The Campaigns of Alexander* (rev. ed). Translated by Aubrey De Sélincourt. London: Penguin Books, 1971.

Bosworth, A.B. *Conquest and Empire: The Reign of Alexander the Great*. Cambridge: CUP, 1988. Reprinted 2006.

———. 'Alexander the Great: Events,' pp. 791–818. In *The Cambridge Ancient History*, 2nd ed, vol. VII, part 1. Edited by F.W. Walbank, A.E. Astin, M.W. Fredriksen, and R.M. Ogilvie. Cambridge: CUP, 1984.

Diodorus Siculus. *Library of History*. Translated by C. Bradford Wells. Cambridge and London: Loeb Classical Library, 1963. Reprinted 2003.

Eddy, Samuel K. *The King is Dead: Studies in Near Eastern Resistance to Hellenism, 334–331 B.C.* Lincoln: University of Nebraska Press, 1961.

Fredricksmeyer, Ernest. 'Alexander, Midas, and the Oracle at Gordium.' pp. 160–168. In *Classical Philology*, LVI: 1961.

Green, Peter. *Alexander the Great, 356–323 B.C.: A Historical Biography*. Berkeley, Los Angeles: University of California Press, 1974. Reprinted 1991.

———. *Alexander to Actium: The Historical Evolution of the Hellenistic Age*. Berkeley: University of California Press, 1990.

Herodotus. *The Histories* (rev. ed). Translated by Aubrey De Sélincourt. London: Penguin Books, 1972.

Justin. *Epitome of the Philippic History of Pompeius Trogus*. Translated by J.C. Yardley. Atlanta: Scholars Press, 1994.

Lane Fox, Robin. *Alexander the Great*. London: Allen Lane, 1973. Updated by Penguin Books (London), 2004.

Mossé, Claude. *Alexander: Destiny and Myth*. Translated by Janet Lloyd. Baltimore: Johns Hopkins, 2004.

Plutarch. *The Age of Alexander*. Translated by Ian Scott-Kilvert. London: Penguin Books, 1973.

Quintus Curtius Rufus. *The History of Alexander*. Trans J.C. Yardley. London: Penguin Books, 1984. Reprinted 2004.

Tarn, W.W. *Alexander the Great, Volume II: Sources and Studies*. Cambridge: CUP, 1948. Reprinted 2002.

Index

Page numbers in *italics* refer to illustrations.

Acesines River 151, 162–3, 167
Achaemenid Empire 19, 24, 27, 34, 53, 67, 100, 181
   see also Persia
Achilles 17, *36*, *52*, 53, 81, 100, 165, 185
Ada, Princess of Caria 75, 185
Aegae, Macedonian capital 8, *9*, 11, 14
Agis III, King of Sparta 104
Agrianian people 58, 107, 108, 119, 145, 152, 167
Ahura Mazda 208
Alexander I Philhellene, King of Macedon 11
Alexander III, King of Macedon
   accession 6, 34, 37–8
   adoption of 75, 85, 185
   ancestry 17, 19, *36*
   Aornos Rock (Pir-Sar), Siege of *148*, 149
   army refuses to continue 164–7
   Babylon *112*, 113–14, 115, 117, 167, 169, 177–8,
      189–90, *191–2*
   and Bessus 125, 127, 129, 132, *133*, 135
   birth 12, 14, 19
   Bucephalus *19*, 20–2, 127, 161–2, *163*, 202
   and Callisthenes 142–3, 144–5, 148
   and Campaspe 69
   Chaeronea, Battle of 6, 28, 30, 33
   childhood 19–20
   cities, founding 97, 162, 166, 181, 193, 194–207, 203,
      211 *see also individual cities*
   death *175*, 176–7, 199, 213
   death of Cleitus the Black *138*, 139, 148
   death of Darius 125, *126*
   death of Hephaestion 174, 176, 213
   Diogenes 39–40
   early campaigns 24
   education 22–4, *25*
   in Egypt 96–7, 101–2, 180–2, 185, 188–9
   empire, extent of *183*, 194, *216*
   Gaugamela, Battle of *85*, 105, 107–8, 110, *111*, 189
   Gaza, Siege of 94–6
   Gordian knot 185–6, *187*
   Granicus, Battle of the 55, 57–60, *61*, 62–4, 67, 68,
      139, 185
   Halicarnassus, Siege of 71–2, 75, 78
   Hydaspes, Battle of the 19, *140*, *150*, 151–61, 166,
      167
   illness 76–7
   illustrations *16*, *24*, *78*, *85*, *91*, *107*, *160*, *178*, *213*, *217*
   India, invasion of 145–69
   Issus, Battle of *54*, 77–9, *80*, 81–3
   letters exchanged with Darius 86, 88, 105

marriages *136*, 139, 171–2, *173*, 214
Miletus, Siege of 71
Multan, Siege of 167
Orientalization of 127, 129, 139
Persepolis 119–20, *121*
Persian Gates, Battle of the 119
plot to murder 129–32, 144
proskynesis (prostration) 129, 139, 141–3, 148
rift with father 30, *31*, 32–4
Sangala, Siege of 163–4
Siwah oracle 97–8, 100–1, 102, 189, 207
Sogdian Rock, Siege of 136–9
succession 204, 213–17
Susa 113, 114, 117–18, 171–2, *173*
and Thalestris 127, *128*
Thebes Revolt *44*, 45
threats to 38–9
and Timoclea *46*
Triballi people 40–1
Tyre, Siege of 87, 89, 91–3, *94*, 188
wounded 63, 82, 96, 139, 149, 167, *168*, 176
Alexander IV, King of Macedon 214, 215
Alexander of Epirus, King of the Molossians *33*, 34
Alexander Sarcophagus *212*
Alexander the Lyncestian 39, 45, 131
Alexandria, Egypt 97, 181, 193, 195–7, *198*, 199–201,
   203, 207
Alexandria in Arachosia 203
Alexandria in Ariana 203
Alexandria in Caucaso 201–2, 203
Alexandria in Margiane 202, 203
Alexandria in Markarene 203
Alexandria in Prophthaisia 203
Alexandria in Susiana 203
Alexandria Iomousa 203
Alexandria on the Jaxartes 203
Alexandria on the Oxus or Alexandria in Tarmita 203
Alexandria Rhambacia 203
Alexandropolis 24
Alexarchos 204, 207
Amanus Mountains 79, 81
Amazon people 127, *128*
Amenhotep III, Pharaoh 98
Ammon 97–8, 167, 197
Amun 97, 98
Amun-Ra 98, 100, *182*
Amyntas, son of Andromenes 58, 67, 119, 131
Amyntas, son of Arrhabaeus 58, 60
Antigonus I Monopthalmus, King 195, 207, 215, 216
Antioch 193, 202, 204, *205–6*
Antiocha in Margiane 202

Antiochus I, Seleucid King 202
Antiochus III the Great, Seleucid King 207–8
Antiochus IV Epiphanes, Seleucid King 208, *210*, 211
Antipater, General 23, 24, 37, 45–6, 101, 131, 132, 177,
   204, 215
Aornos Rock (Pir-Sar), Siege of (327 BCE) *148*, 149
Apelles 69, 70
Apis bull-god 97, 180, 182, 185, *190*
Apollo 92, 207
Arbela 113, *114*
Archelaus I, King of Macedon 11
Ares 60
Argaeus 13–14
Argos 9, 78, 188
Ariamazes 138–9
Aristogeiton *113*, 117
Aristonus 214
Aristotle, education of Alexander 22–4, *25*, 185
armour 49, 50, 67, *106*, 107
Arrhabaeus the Lyncestian 39, 58
Arrian
   Alexander in Egypt 96, 101, 189
   Bucephalus 161, 162
   Cleitus the Black 139
   death of Alexander 177, 213
   Gaugamela, Battle of 105
   Gedrosian Desert 169, 171
   Gordian knot 185, 187
   Granicus, Battle of the 58, 59, 62, 64, 67
   illness of Alexander 76
   India, invasion of 148, 152, 156, 160, 164, 165, 166,
      167
   Sogdian Rock, Siege of 137, 138
Arsinoe II, Princess 207
Arsites of Phrygia 55, 57, 67, 185
Artabazus, General 127, 136, 172
Artacama 172
Artaxerxes III Ochus, Great King of Persia 24, 27, 88,
   180
Artaxerxes IV, Arses, Great King of Persia 88
Artaxerxes V Bessus, Great King of Persia 127
Artemesia II, Queen of Caria 75
Artemis, Temple of 19, *66*, *68*, 70, 185
Asclepius *55*, 78, 174
Asia Minor 23, 24, 27, 33, 67, 181, 215
Athena 53, 67, 185, 186
Attalus, General 32, 33, 34, 38, 39, 46
Attalus, son of Andromenes 37
Augustus, Emperor of Rome *215*
Azimilik, King of Tyre 92

Ba'al 92, 98, *117*
Babylon
   Alexander in *112*, 113–14, 115, 116, 117, 167, 169,
      177–8, 189–90, *191–2*
   gods of 208
   Siege of (522 BCE) 179
Bacchus *147*, 148
Bactrian people 108, 113, 127, 135, 136, 172
Bagophanes 114, 115
Bajaur Valley 145, 149
Balkans 9, 46, 107
Bardylis, King of Illyria 14, 38
battering rams 71
Bel-Marduk 179–80, 189–90, *192*
Bessus, General 108, 113, 123, 125, 127, 129, 132, *133*,
   135
boar hunts 12, 143–4
Bucephala 162, 166, 202, *203*
Bucephalus *19*, 20–2, 63–4, 70, 127, *161*, *178*, *217*
   death of 153, 155, 161–2, *163*, 202
Byblos, Phoenicia 86, *90*, 102
Byzantium 24, 38

Calas, son of Harpalus 58, 67
Callisthenes 142–3, 144–5, 148
Cambyses II, Great King of Persia 100, *101*, 180
Campaspe 69
Canopus, Egypt 97, 196, 201
Cappadocia 186
Caria 33, 75, 185
Carmania 169, 171
Carthage 87, 89, 92–3
Cassander 23, 207
catapults 70–1, 92, 96
Cebalinus 130
Chaerona, Battle of (338 BCE) 6, 27–8, *29*, 30, 33,
   39
Chares 144
chariots *51*, *82*, 105, 107, 108, 153, 156
Chios 75
Cilician Gates 186
Cimon, General 98
Cleander, General 131
Cleitus, King of Illyria 38, 41–2
Cleitus the Black *62*, *63*, 107, 141, 165
   death of *138*, 139, 148
Cleomenes 199
Cleopatra, wife of Philip II 13, 32, 33, 39, 41
Coenus 58, 131, 136, 156, 165, 167
Congress of Corinth (337 BCE) 30

Craterus
  Alexander's succession 215–16
  Babylon 169, 171
  Granicus, Battle of the 58
  India, invasion of 149, 152, 153, 159–60, 167
  infantry commander 135
  Persian Gates, Battle of the 119
  Philotas 131
Cyprus 87, 91, 94, 104
Cyrus II, Great King of Persia 100, 101, 118, 179, 180

Darius I, Great King of Persia 119, 179
Darius III, Great King of Persia 77
  Alexander's invasion and 53
  death 123, 125, 126
  Demosthenes 38
  escape of 113–14
  Gaugamela, Battle of 85, 105, 107–8, 110, 111, 151, 189
  Issus, Battle of 54, 79, 81–3
  letters exchanged with Darius 86, 88, 105
  treasure 117
Dascylium 67, 68, 186
Deinocrates of Rhodes 195, 196, 197
Demaratus of Corinth 62–3
Demetrius 130, 131
Demetrius, son of Pythonax 142, 143, 152
Demetrius I the Besieger, King of Macedon 207
Demetrius the Athenian 199–200
Demosthenes 27–8, 37–8
Diogenes of Sinope 39–40
Dionysus 12, 17, 42, 139, 146, 148, 165, 171, 185, 207–8
diving bell 104
Drypetis 172

Ecbatana 123, 124, 125, 131, 174, 208
The Education of Alexander (Marsyas) 23–4
Egypt
  Alexander in 96–7, 101–2, 180–2, 185, 189
  Persian invasion 180
elephants 105, 151, 153, 155–6, 157–8, 160, 164
Epaminondas 14, 49
Ephesus 19, 67–8, 70, 185
Epirus 12, 32, 46
Eumenes 172, 214, 216
Euphrates River 104–5, 106
Euripides 11, 22, 146, 148, 199

Galatia 186
gastraphetes 'belly-shooter' catapult 71
Gaugamela, Battle of (331 BCE) 85, 105, 107–8, 109, 110, 111, 114, 151, 189
Gaza, Siege of (332 BCE) 94–6
Gedrosia 169, 170, 171
Glaucias 174

god-kings 207–8, 210
Gonzaga Cameo 207
Gordium, Phrygia 185–6, 187
Granicus, Battle of the (334 BCE) 55, 57–60, 61, 62–4, 67, 68, 139, 185
Great Sphinx of Giza 181

Hagnon, General 17, 19
Halicarnassus 12, 73–4
  Siege of (334 BCE) 71–2, 75, 78
Harmodius 113, 117
Harpalus 23, 33, 104, 105, 167
Hecataeus 39
Hellenistic period (323–31 BCE) 193–4, 204, 207, 208, 211
Hellespont 53
Hellespontine Phrygia 67
Hephaestion 174
  death of 174, 176, 213
  Gaza, Siege of 94
  India, invasion of 145, 149, 151, 152, 167
  mistaken for Alexander 85, 87
Heracles 17, 19, 42, 78, 86, 93, 98, 100, 149, 167, 185, 188
Herodotus 9, 11, 17, 56, 179, 180, 185
Heromenes the Lyncestian 39
Hindu Kush mountains 132, 145, 194, 201
hipparchies, cavalry 135
Hipparchus 113, 117
The Histories (Herodotus) 9, 11, 56, 179
Homer 22, 37, 53, 197
hoplites 17, 18, 28, 47
Horus 182
hunting 11–12, 143–4, 174
Hydaspes, Battle of the (326 BCE) 19, 140, 150, 151–61, 166, 167
Hydraotes River 167
Hyksos people 98, 102
Hyphasis River 164, 166, 167, 171
Hyrcania 125, 127

Iliad (Homer) 22, 37
Illyria 9, 13, 14, 33, 41–2
India
  Aornos Rock (Pir-Sar), Siege of 148, 149
  Hydaspes, Battle of the 19, 140, 150, 151–61, 166, 167
  invasion of 145–69
  Multan, Siege of 167
  Sangala, Siege of 163–4
Indus River 149, 150, 151
Issus, Battle of (333 BCE) 54, 77–9, 80, 81–3, 123

Jerusalem 95, 97, 208, 210, 211

Khyber Pass 145
Kunar Valley 145–6

larnax coffin 8
League of Corinth 6, 38, 39, 45, 71
Leonnatus 37, 135, 142, 169, 216
Leuctra, Battle of (371 BCE) 6, 15, 28
Libya 97–8, 99, 100–1, 102, 103, 189
Lighthouse of Pharos 196, 198
lion hunts 12, 174
Lydia 67, 146
Lysander 17, 19, 98

Maccabean Rebellion 208
Macedonia
  early history 9, 11–12
  empire, extent of 183, 194, 216
  ethnicity of people 8–9, 11
  India, invasion of 145–69
  rise of 6, 8, 38
  ships 50, 51, 53, 70, 71, 87, 94, 96, 166–7, 168
  trade 8, 194, 196, 199
Macedonian army
  casualties 59, 64, 66, 91, 93, 164, 171
  Companion cavalry 46, 49, 50, 57–8, 63, 68, 82–3, 107, 110, 135
  corps of engineers 71, 87, 93
  logistics of 47, 49–50
  phalanx 41, 43, 48, 65, 108, 110, 155–6, 158
  Royal Squadron 107, 108, 119, 130, 145, 153, 167
  Silver Shields 135, 145, 149, 152, 167
  strength 47, 79, 101
  tactics 57–9, 79, 105, 107–8, 119, 152–3, 155–6
Mausoleum of Halicarnassus 74, 75
Mazaeus, General 108, 110, 114, 117, 189, 213
Media 113, 114, 123, 172
Meleager, General 59, 214–15
Melqart 86, 92, 93, 102, 188, 189
Memnon of Rhodes
  death 75
  Granicus, Battle of the 55, 57, 60, 62, 63, 64, 68
  Halicarnassus, Siege of 71–2
Memphis, Egypt 97, 101, 180, 189, 190, 195, 199, 208
Menidas, General 101, 131
mercenaries 63–4, 77, 81, 82, 83, 101, 107, 127
Mesopotamia 180, 181
Methone, Siege of (ca. 354 BCE) 27
Midas, King of Phrygia 184, 185
Mieza, Macedon 22–3, 25, 185
Miletus, Siege of (334 BCE) 71
Mithridates, General 62–3
Molossian people 12–13
Multan, Siege of (326 BCE) 167

Nearchus the Cretan 24, 33, 70, 167, 169, 171, 172
Neoptolemus I, King of the Molossians 12–13
Nicaea 162, 166, 202, 203
Nicanor 58, 107
Nicomachus 130, 131
Nineveh 105, 208
Nysa, India 145–6, 148

Olympias (mother of Alexander) 12–13, 14, 32, 33, 34, 37, 41, 100, 172, 215
Olympus, Mount 10, 11
Oxus River 132, 135, 203
Oxyartes 136, 138, 139, 172

Panjshir Valley (Valley of the Five Lions) 201–2
Parmenion, General
  Alexander's succession 38, 39
  death of 131–2
  death of son 102, 104
  Gaugamela, Battle of 105, 107, 108, 114
  Granicus, Battle of the 57, 58, 59–60, 62
  invasion of Persia 46, 67, 68, 77, 86, 185
  Issus, Battle of 78, 82, 83
Pausanias, General 19
Pausanias of Orestis 6, 34, 35, 37, 38
Pausanias (pretender to Macedonian throne) 13
Pella, Macedon 11, 24, 26
Pellium, Illyria 41–2
Peloponnesian War (431–404 BCE) 17
Pelusium, Egypt 96–7
Perdiccas, General 119
  Granicus, Battle of the 58
  hipparch 135
  India, invasion of 145, 149, 152, 167
  pledges support to Alexander 46–7
  regent, acts as 119, 213–16
Perdiccas I, King of Macedon 9, 11
Perdiccas II, King of Macedon 11
Perdiccas III, King of Macedon 13, 38
Perinthus, Siege of (340 BCE) 24, 71, 72
Persepolis 119–20, 121–2, 125, 180, 208, 209, 210
Perseus 98, 100, 189
Persia
  Alexander invades 53
  Gaugamela, Battle of 85, 105, 107–8, 109, 110, 111, 114, 151, 189
  Gaza, Siege of 94–6
  Granicus, Battle of the 55, 57–60, 61, 62–4, 67, 68, 139, 185
  Halicarnassus, Siege of 71–2, 75, 78
  Issus, Battle of 54, 77–9, 80, 81–3
  Miletus, Siege of 71
  Persian Gates, Battle of the 119
  Plataea, Battle of 17, 18

revolts in empire 24, 27
Salamis, Battle of 56
ships 53, 56, 70, 71, 77
Sogdian Rock, Siege of 136–9
trade 86
treasure taken from 210–11
Tyre, Siege of 87, 89, 91–3, *94*, 188
Persian army *58, 63*
casualties 64
strength 57, 60, 79
tactics 57, 60, 62, 82, 107–8
Persian Gates, Battle of the (330 BCE) 119, *120*
Pharos Island 196, 197, *198*
Philip Arrhidaeus 19, 33, 214, 215
Philip II, King of Macedon *6, 14*
accession 13–14
Asia Minor 23, 24, 27, 33, 38
assassination 6, 34, *35*, 37
Athens and 27–8, 30
Chaerona, Battle of 6, 27–8, *29*, 30, 39
marriage 12–13
military reforms 49, 70–1, 151, 165
Perinthus, Siege of 24, 71, 72
rift with Alexander 30, *31*, 32–4
Philotas 46, *47*, 57–8, 78, 119, 129–31
Phoenicia 86, 181
ships 87, 89, 91, *94*, 104
Tyre, Siege of 87, 89, 91–3, *94*, 188

Phrygia 67, 146, 181, 185–6, 215
Pinarus River *79, 80*, 81, 82, 83
Plataea, Battle of (479 BCE) 17, *18*
Plutarch 13, 19, 21, 100, 125, 131–2, 197
Pompeii *54*
Porus, King of Parauva 151–3, *154*, 155–6, *157*, 159–60, 164
Poseidon 167, 208
Prodromoi cavalry 58, 60
proskynesis (prostration) 129, 139, 141–3, 148
Ptah, Egyptian god 97
Ptolemaic monarchies 194, 196, 199, 208, 210–11, 216
Ptolemy I Soter, King of Egypt *199*
Alexander's succession 214, 216
Alexandria 199–200
capture of Bessus 132, 135
Halicarnassus, Siege of 75, 78
India, invasion of 146, 152
punished by Philip II 33–4
Thebes Revolt 45
Tyre, Siege of 92
Ptolemy II Philadelphus, King of Egypt 200, 207
Ptolemy III Eurgetes, King of Egypt 208

Ramses II, Pharaoh 98
Rhacotis, Egypt 196, 201
Rhodes 87, 94
Roxane (wife of Alexander) *136*, 139, 172, 177, 213, 214

Sacred Band, Theban 6, 28, 30, 33
Sangala, Siege of (326 BCE) 163–4
Sardis *66, 67*
sarissa spear 49, 50, 58, 62, *65, 106*, 107, 156
satraps 55, 67, 71–2, 104, 114, 117, 185
Seleucia on the Tigris 207
Seleucid monarchies 194, 204, 207, 208, 211
Seleucus I Nicator, Seleucid King 152, 172, 195, 202, 204, 207, 214
Semiramis, Queen 169, 171
Shipka Pass 40–1
siegecraft 70–1, 72, 87, 89, 149, 151
Sisygambis, mother of Darius 83, 85–6, *87*, 110, 117–18
Siwah, Libya 97–8, *99*, 100–1, 102, *103*, 189, 207
slavery 64, 93
Sogdian Rock, Siege of (327 BCE) 136, *137*, 138–9
Sogdiana 132, *134*, 136
Soli 77–8, 186
Sparta 6, *15*, 27, 46, 104
Spitamenes 132, 135, 136, 172
Spithridates *62, 63*
Stateira, Princess 105, 171, 214
Stateira, Queen 83, 123
Successors, the (*Diadochoi*) 162, 207, 208, 210, 211, 216–17
Susa 67, 113, 114, 117–18, 210
mass marriage in 171–2, *173*
Swat Valley 145, 149, 151

Syria 86, 104, 105, 181, 204
Syrmus, King of the Triballi 41

Tarsus 76–7, 117, 186
Taxiles 151, 159
Teos, Ionia 207–8
Thais 120, *121*
Thalestris, Queen of the Amazons 127, *128*
Thebes 6, *15*, 27, 28, 30, 33, *46*
Themistocles, Admiral 56
Theo Adelphoi (Sibling Gods) 207–8
Thessalian people 6, 11, 28, 58, 76, 82, 107
Thrace 9, 24, 38–9, 76, 82, 101, 107
Thutmoses III, Pharaoh 98, *102*
Tigris River *106*, 181, 207
torsion catapult (*katapeltai*) 70–1, 92, *96*
trade 8, 86, 194, 196, 199
Triballi people 27, 38–9, 40–1
Trojan War (1250–1200 BCE) 53
Tyrannicides, The *113*, 117
Tyre, Phoenicia 86–7, *94, 95*, 102, 104, 123, *189*
Siege of (332 BCE) 87, 89, 91–3, *94*, 188

Xerxes I, King of Persia 6, 117, 119, 120, 179–80, 189

Zeus 11, 67, 98, 101, 146, 148, 185, 186
Zeus-Ammon 98, 162, *179*, 189

Picture Credits